P9-CDH-772

the ant and the
ELEPHANT

LEADERSHIP FOR THE SELF

A Parable and 5-Step Plan to Transform Individual Performance

by Vince Poscente

LIBRETTO
PUBLISHING

Notice:
This book is a work of fiction. Names, characters, businesses,
organizations, places, events and incidents are either a product
of the author's imagination or are used fictitiously.
Any resemblance to actual persons, living or dead, events,
or locales is entirely coincidental.

Copyright ©2006 Vince Poscente

ISBN: 1-893430-14-6

Library of Congress Control Number: 2004106893

All rights reserved under all Copyright Conventions.

No part of this book may be reproduced, stored in a retrieval
system, or transmitted by any means, electronic, mechanical,
photocopying, recording, or otherwise, without written
permission from the author.

Submit all requests for reprinting to:
Greenleaf Book Group LP
4425 Mopac South, Suite 600
Longhorn Bldg., 3rd Floor
Austin, TX 78735
(512) 891-6100

Published in the United States by
Libretto Publishing
Dallas, TX

www.librettopublishing.com

Layout by Francine Smith
Cover design by Mark Dame, Dame Creative

Printed in the United States of America

First Edition

08 07 06 05   9 8 7 6 5 4 3

Dedicated to my parents for their leadership,
mentorship and love.

To my mother, a beacon of perpetual curiosity, and in
memory of my father, the definition of steadfast integrity.

In honor of my wife, who is my best friend and
greatest teacher. And to our children, Max, Alexia and
Isabella, for leading me to an "oasis" of joy.

Contents

Leadership for the Self

• • •

Before anyone can reach his full potential as a leader, he must first be a leader to himself.* He must capitalize on innate talents and strengths, challenge the habits that hinder his growth and manage the fears and negative emotions that frequently keep him from realizing his goals.

As you know, our minds function in two distinct spaces—conscious and subconscious thought. Our "ant" is the intentional part of the brain—it houses our critical, analytical thoughts. Our "elephant," however, is the instinctual, impulsive part of the brain—it houses emotions and memories and even guides the body to perform its vital functions. While we tend to know our conscious minds—or *ants*—rather well, we often overlook the power of our *elephantine* subconscious minds. Unfortunately, when we do, we squander a wellspring of human potential.

Imagine a tiny ant on the back of a massive African elephant. No matter how diligently that ant marches east, if the elephant he sits upon travels in the opposite direction, the ant will end up even farther west than his starting point. Similarly, we will find ourselves receding from our goals if our conscious and subconscious minds are not aligned. What elephant-like aspects of our personalities hold us back from meeting challenges? How do our emotions get in the way of our ability to act and communicate effectively? What does it truly mean to commit to realize a dream?

* Generic male identifiers (such as "he") =
she/he/her/him/hers/his/herself/himself . . . Whew!

A good leader may recognize that he indulges elephant-like habits that keep him shy of his goal—but a *great* leader does something about it. He confronts the behaviors and routines that keep his subconscious stuck. He works to refashion deep-seated beliefs, attitudes and truths so that they support his conscious efforts. The *great* leader conquers his hidden fears, antes up and makes an emotional investment in his vision to show others the way to success.

The Ant and the Elephant is an entertaining parable to help you do just that. Its goal is to demonstrate how we can unite the powerful forces of conscious and subconscious thought to reach our peak performance levels as individuals *and* as corporate leaders.

1

Leaving the Familiar Behind

Many years ago in the African savannah, something extraordinary happened. An ant no larger than a drop of rain, found the strength, power and determination he needed to move a gigantic elephant.

It isn't possible, you say! There is simply no way an ant could move an elephant.

But every word of this story is true.* Through months upon months of dogged self-searching, an overly conscious ant named Adir learned how to harness the power of his elephant-sized subconscious teammate, Elgo. In the process, he not only learned about himself, but he also discovered what it took to become a leader worth following.

Of course, no ant—or man, for that matter—is an island. Were it not for the patient coaching of a wise old owl called Brio—whose voice sounds eerily similar to James Earl Jones's*—Adir's dreams of a better future may never have been realized. With Brio's help, however, Adir discovered

* *Wink, wink.*
* Think Mufasa, not Darth Vader.

what it means to be a leader to himself. More importantly, he learned how this crucial self-knowledge would allow him to become a leader to others.

Adir and Elgo changed the direction and course of their lives. After hearing what Brio had to tell Adir and Elgo, you could change the direction of your life, too.

It is an exceptional story.

An *inspirational* story.

One from which I know you can benefit.

And it begins with a tremendous storm . . .

• • •

Late one night, as Adir was sleeping peacefully in his bed, his friend Charlie woke him.

"Adir! Adir!" Charlie gasped, shaking him. "A bad storm has rolled in. We need to make sure the provisions are protected!" Adir, who had been in the throes of a juicy dream, grumpily rose from bed. He rubbed his eyes open and followed Charlie out of the anthill.

Once outside, Adir could see that the entire colony had been called upon to help in this important effort. Adir watched as his friends and colleagues scurried about, trying to move the food and supplies from the wind-swept terrain to protective cover. As they worked, the rain and wind picked up. It didn't take Adir long to realize that the situation was pure chaos. Many of his co-workers were running around in circles like ants with their heads cut off.*

"You're going the wrong way!" Adir called to them. He scrambled to a high ridge and, trying to project his voice over the howl of the wind, shouted, "Follow me! This way will be easier!" No matter how loudly Adir shouted, however, his fellow ants wouldn't follow his lead. He strained his voice

* Or chickens. You get the idea.

and tried to get their attention by waving his four front legs—but they were either not paying attention to him or flat out ignoring him.

Suddenly, an enormous bolt of lightning illuminated the sky. In that moment, Adir paused to look at his colony. The electrifying flash captured the pandemonium; it was as though the whole colony were standing frozen in time.

This was the last Adir would see of his colony for many months. For the next thing the little ant knew, an amazing gust of wind had swept him upward into the sky. Adir felt as though he were flying as he sailed and tumbled through the air. When that gust died down, another replaced it. And then another. And another.

The rain continued to beat down upon the dry earth, and winds continued to whistle across the plains. There was no telling how far adrift Adir had gone, and in the pitch-dark night and torrential rainstorm he completely lost his bearings. When the wind finally deposited him on the ground, Adir scurried to the safety afforded by a shallow ravine. His weathered body collapsed, and he fell into a deep, deep slumber.

Little did Adir know that his life would be changed forever by that storm. It had taken him from the creature comforts of his colony and given him the chance to see his life anew. In fact, if it hadn't been for that terrifying storm, Adir never would have discovered the Oasis.

• • •

Adir awoke to the calm following the previous night's storm feeling—among other things—somewhat *confused.* He rubbed his eyes, yawned and realized almost immediately that his surroundings were completely unfamiliar. The terror of the previous night came back to him, and he immediately started to feel anxious and sick in the pit of his stomach. He looked around, but saw none of his fellow ants. In fact, he didn't see the slightest bit of evidence that his colony had ever existed. He scouted the terrain close by, but couldn't even detect a trail that would lead him home.*

Emptiness consumed him. He felt incredibly alone and defeated. The reality of his situation set in as quickly as the sun rises in the African savannah. Without his colony, Adir did not know what to do with himself, much less how he would fill his days and nights. Perhaps the scariest thing of all, though, was that without his colony, Adir had no mission or purpose. He gazed into a shimmering puddle of rainwater, the only remnant of the storm from the night before. As he studied his reflection, he realized that without his colony, he wasn't quite certain who *he* was.

The question of purpose echoed in Adir's mind. What had been his purpose in the colony? He contemplated the notion endlessly—after all, what else was he to do in this barren place all by himself?

Throughout that first day alone, Adir felt his little brain throb. He was distressed.

Before being separated from the colony, Adir could safely say that he did his job well. By all accounts, he was reliable and dependable. The other ants knew he was a good ant with good intentions and a willingness to work hard. Recently, the Queen had even promoted him to a position that made him responsible for a whole delegation of ants. But in truth, Adir hadn't felt comfortable in the role. More often than not, when Adir gave an instruction, his workforce would stare at him with those empty ant eyes, not quite sure

---

* This is one of those stories in which ants can talk, but they don't have access to mapquest.com.

what to do with the information. It seemed too hard, too impossible, to try to inspire them. He didn't know how to effectively communicate his vision to them. Sometimes, when he tried to get his team enthused about a certain task, he couldn't help but feel like a phony. Sure, he could talk a good game, but he never really believed what came out of his mouth. Needless to say, it hadn't been going well. Just the week before, the Queen pulled Adir into her nest to tell him his delegation was "under performing." Adir had better figure out a way to "get things together," she said in her superior way, or there would be "consequences."

Now, alone and separated from his friends and colleagues, Adir was able to be honest with himself: he never really felt invested in the outcome of the colony.* This troubled him. He knew that he had a great deal to offer the world. Indeed, he knew he had a great deal to offer his fellow ants, especially his workforce. Maybe if he tried harder, he would make the colony a better place to live and work—but what did that mean? How should he try harder, and at *what*, exactly? He sat upright and cast his gaze into the distance. He took a good look around and felt the promise of great things drain from his body.

"Isn't that just the way?" he muttered, stomping one of his little feet. "As soon as I realize I could have done better, it's too late. Oh, heck! Who am I kidding? I'll never find my colony! And even if I do, I can't change anything, especially the ant I am . . . "

Adir's body slumped down once again. Defeated. Hopeless. Downright beleaguered.

• • •

5

---

* Excluding the stock options, of course.

Time passed, and a tedious routine began to fill his days. It seemed to Adir that everything he did was to ensure his survival—nothing more, nothing less. Gone were the days of socializing with his friends and colleagues at break time. As a solitary ant, there was always a great deal to do, and yet he often felt like he was just going through the motions to get through each day.

Every morning he performed his usual routine. He groomed each leg and his entire body, gave his antennae a thorough combing and brushed his pincers. He readied himself for the usual lifting—fifty times his body weight— and sadly, without even realizing it, he became accustomed to the harsh environment and his loneliness.

Although it was a struggle, Adir was still able to find food in his unforgiving surroundings. As he searched high and low for his next meal, he often looked into the distance, noting how the dreary land contrasted with the startling blue of the sky. Inevitably, the vista filled him with a sense of longing and regret, and these feelings persisted, nagging him long into the night. *There must be more to life than this*, he thought as he watched the sparkling stars. *Life should be a fulfilling journey, not just a struggle to survive.*

Life should be a fulfilling journey, not just a struggle to survive.

Then, one afternoon, a large crow swooped down beside him and began to peck away at the stash of food Adir had collected. Given that the bird was a thousand times larger than he, Adir decided to approach the crow cautiously.

"Excuse me," Adir said in his loudest non-confrontational voice. "Um, sir, I believe you're eating my food."

The bird looked up with one stony eye that sent a shudder through Adir's little body. "*And? So?* Are you going to do something about it?"

"Oh, no, no, no . . . " Adir said apologetically, "I just wanted to . . . errr . . . make sure you were enjoying it; that's all."

"Thanks," the bird cackled and sneered, "but no thanks. I'm on my way to the Oasis, and the food there is better than what you've got here. You can keep it."

Adir's antennae stiffened with interest. "The Oasis? What's that? I've never heard of the Oasis . . . "

"You don't know *the Oasis*?"* The bird laughed, "Ha! What a joke! The Oasis is only the best place in the whole world; that's all. It's like paradise. In fact, it's better than paradise; it's like *heaven*. Everything you could ever dream of—coconuts, papayas, mangos—*they just drip right off the trees*. It's the land of sunshine and lush green fields. Best of all, it's the place where everything just flows . . . whatever you dream of or want, it *happens* in the Oasis." The crow's eyes twinkled at the very thought of this magical place until he realized that Adir was staring at him, and he quickly shook himself out of his reverie. Surveying Adir's surroundings, he added snidely, "Sure isn't like this place; that's for sure!"

"It sounds *amazing!*" Adir said. "Are you going there now?"

"You bet your bottom I am." The bird turned his back and prepared for takeoff.

"Will you take me? Or, at least . . . um . . . tell me how to get there?" squeaked Adir.

7

---

* Crows, apparently, are snobs.

The black crow cocked his head over his wings and winked. "And precisely *why*, little ant, would I do that?"

With that, the crow flew away.*

• • •

After hearing the crow describe the Oasis, Adir became consumed by the very thought of it. In fact, he dreamt of the Oasis day and night. *What is it like?* he wondered. *What is this magical land really like? Is it a land of sunshine, blue skies and opportunity? Will I find my fellow ants there? Surely I will. If the crow is right and the Oasis is like paradise, then the good life I want—a life that will take me beyond the daily grind of survival—is there, just waiting for me.*

If he could find a way to get there, he was positive all of his dreams would come true and all of his problems would be solved. Reaching the Oasis became his goal, his mission, his most passionate dream.

Adir felt better than he had in months. Maybe there was a positive side to his separation from the colony. Maybe the storm had taken him from his old comfort zone and plopped him in a new world, just brimming with possibilities. The only question Adir had now was how in the world he could turn that dream into a reality.

* If ants had fingers, our little hero would have given that bird *the* bird.

2

Following the Same Old Path

It is common knowledge that elephants have great memories, and Elgo the elephant was no exception to the rule. He remembered *everything* he ever experienced, from the taste of the grass he had eaten as a small calf to the way yesterday's hot sun had beaten down upon his back. In fact, it was his extraordinary memory that maintained the consistent rhythm of his legs moving up and down in a machine-like motion (whether he knew where he was headed or not). No matter what it was—a sight, a smell, a motion, a sound or even a touch—it lingered in Elgo's mind and memory forever. He was a walking storehouse of memories, habits and instincts.

Elgo was a strong elephant with enormous shoulders and a powerful flank.* There was very little Elgo couldn't plow right through on his travels. And yet, despite his strength and might, Elgo was surprisingly very timid. Perhaps this was because of the environment in which he

---

* Elephants are sensitive about weight issues, so let's just say Elgo had a "significant following." He was large and in charge.

had grown up. He had been guided by two loving parents throughout his formative years who, without knowing it, may have soured him on life.

Elgo's father was notorious for his pessimism and spent his days and nights telling anyone who would listen how hard life was. As fathers are known to do, Elgo's dad would often lecture the young elephant: "The terrain we live in is unforgiving. I pray you will never know the hardship of the Great Drought, but even if you don't, you will see that life is a struggle."

Elgo's mother had taken very good care of him when he was young, but she was equally cautious. She always reminded him to be safe and not to stray from the established path of the elephant herd. "Danger lurks at every bend, and you must be careful," she would say in her low, soothing voice. "Be a good elephant and do what you're told to do. Listen to your father—he knows best."

Elgo heeded their advice and warnings. Alongside his father and mother, he learned to work hard and to protect his territory. As he matured, he learned about all the limitations that elephants faced. Coping, struggling, accepting—this was every elephant's lot in life, and Elgo never forgot it.

Of course, though Elgo was obedient, there was a part of him that lived outside of the confines of the herd. Even as a calf he had loved to daydream, and he always found peace in escaping reality and drifting away in his imagination.

In Elgo's youth, his uncle would tell him of a wonderful, faraway land where there were deep, clear pools of water, luscious green trees, sweet-smelling flowers and other friendly animals. In this paradise, there was no searching for food, water or shade. Everything an elephant needed to be happy was just a short walk away.*

10

---

* At the Happy Elephant store. Attention, E-Mart shoppers: there is a blue-light special on bliss.

"In the Oasis," his uncle would say, "there is no walking mile after mile searching for water and no digging in the dusty ground we see here. It's easy living, and everyone," he smiled at Elgo, "is happy there."

Unfortunately, each time his uncle began to share his stories about the Oasis, Elgo's father would butt in.

"Don't listen to that nonsense!" his father would trumpet from behind. "Your uncle is only pulling your trunk. Life is tough; it's hard, Elgo. And if you don't believe me now, just you wait; you'll see how hard it can be." Then, his father would typically turn to Elgo's uncle and say, "Tell him the truth. Tell him how hard life is! Don't mislead him!"

Elgo's uncle would sigh heavily. "It's true," he would say, looking at Elgo's father. "An elephant's life is tough . . . even when it doesn't have to be."

11

Life is **tough**, even when it doesn't have to be.

• • •

Like all male elephants, Elgo left his mother's herd when he was fully grown. Although he knew this was for the best, he missed the safety and innocence of his youth. On one particular morning, as Elgo trudged along the well-worn elephant path, he looked up into the sky and wondered what it would be like to be a cloud. *Imagine that*, he mused, *sailing freely across the sky. How wonderful that would be! What would the savannah look like from way up there, I wonder?* Then he held his ears straight out, away from his body, cooling himself as the hot sun rose higher in the sky.

But it didn't take long for Elgo to snap back into reality. He lowered his head to the ground and grabbed a trunk full of dried weeds. Then he returned to his long, tedious march, always searching for the next watering hole and food along the way.

Every so often, Elgo couldn't help but imagine the faraway land he had heard of as a young elephant. He didn't want to admit it to himself, but he had actually begun to think of the Oasis as his home. It was where he *felt* he belonged. Of course, getting there was another matter. Elgo had accepted long ago that the Oasis might as well be renamed the Mirage. He would never see it. *Fantasize all you like*, he told himself, *but the Oasis exists only in your mind.*

He continued to do what he had been told to do during his early years. Echoes of his mother's voice bounced around in his mind: "Be a good elephant and do what you are told."* That was all there was to it: follow the path that has been laid out before you, and don't bother asking questions. The elephant's life, after all, is very hard.

● ● ●

Of course, such behavior is not exclusive to elephants. The world is full of creatures that want one thing, but can never seem to break the pattern of negative habits that keep them from realizing their dreams. There was one creature in the savannah who knew this from many years of experience. His name was Brio the Wise Owl, a legend throughout the

---

* You know . . . Eat your vegetables . . . Clean your room . . . Don't stick your trunk out at me . . . I gestated you for twenty-two months and gave birth to a 265-pound baby—don't talk back to me.

savannah for his remarkable intelligence and timeless teachings. Brio had known Elgo's parents for many years and could recognize Elgo's powerful carriage and broad shoulders from miles away. He also knew a great deal about the pessimistic upbringing Elgo had received.

As Elgo trudged on, the beautiful spotted owl gracefully rode the currents high above the elephant's head. To Brio, it seemed almost inevitable that Elgo would continue to travel away from the Oasis without even knowing it.

"That poor elephant doesn't even know *how* to change directions," Brio said in his thick, robust voice. "Despite all the clues—the running water and green grasslands in the distance—he still doesn't notice." Brio flew to a high branch and sighed, "Like so many other creatures, the direction of the Oasis escapes him."

Little did Elgo know that Brio was watching him from high above, plotting his new direction.

13

3

Discovering the Possibilities

Ever since Adir met the crow, the mere idea of the Oasis had consumed him. And yet, like so many of us, Adir saw the distance between his dream and his day-to-day reality as an insurmountable obstacle.

He went to bed each night with the intention of setting off in the direction of his dreams at daybreak, but by the time he woke, he was too frightened to go anywhere. Unfortunately, Adir let doubt creep into his mind and make a home there. He wondered whether the crow had been telling him the truth—was the Oasis really as good as he claimed? More importantly, how would he ever be able to get there? In which direction should he travel? How long would it take him? Would he be able to make the journey all by himself? Would it be dangerous?*

His life went on the same, day after day, night after night. It was hard to ignore the simple fact: he wasn't making any progress. He couldn't help but feel his dream of

* Psst! Adir is a little neurotic.

reaching the Oasis slipping away. *Maybe I should just resign myself to my miserable life,* he thought. *It's not great—heck, it's not even good—but at least it's tolerable.*

. . .

Adir knew that ants had destinies, but he didn't know his own. Destiny was a concept that confused him. Actually, it's a concept that confuses most of us. Although he didn't know it at the time, Adir was not alone.

One day, as Adir was slogging along with a blizzard of positive and negative thoughts whirling in his head, he gradually became very agitated. He knew what he wanted, but it was as if his willpower and determination were evaporating. The Oasis was becoming harder to imagine. The small ant became increasingly upset as he wondered about his destiny in life. His emotions spun out of control. His frustration suddenly reached a boiling point, and in a moment of weakness, he blurted out, "What the heck is my destiny, anyway!?!"

The question hung in the wind and echoed across the gray landscape. Then, a deep, rumbling voice that seemed to come out of nowhere responded to him.

"Indeed! What *is* your destiny?"

Oh, my gosh, thought Adir, gripping his head in anxiety. *I'm losing my mind. I've heard of hallucinations, but this is ridiculous. I've definitely been alone for way too long, and isn't this fabulous . . . now I'm talking to myself!*

"You're not talking to yourself, little ant," said the voice.

"Ah! Who said that?" said Adir nervously as he looked all around, convinced he was going cuckoo.*

The sunshine, which had previously been warming Adir's jet-black body, was suddenly blocked. He shook with fear, squinted into the light, and—expecting to see a creature with

---

* Is "going cuckoo" lame? If so, please feel free to substitute the following clever alternatives:

  A) One sandwich short of a picnic

  B) Depriving some village of an idiot

  C) In the great storeroom of life, not all his fruit jars are on the shelf

  D) All of the above

a physical dominance to match the massive, penetrating voice—instead saw the portly silhouette of Brio the Wise Owl.

• • •

As a young ant, Adir had heard stories—legends, really—about Brio, but he had never met him personally. Brio was well known for helping many creatures in the savannah learn valuable lessons. Rumors circulated all around the savannah about how Brio had single-handedly saved the mango industry from going bankrupt, and that he'd successfully negotiated a land settlement between two packs of loud-mouthed hyenas.

Adir couldn't help but recall the old adage, "When the ant is ready, the owl will appear." He just *had* to be Brio's next student. With a force that nearly overwhelmed him, Adir realized that Brio's teachings could help him achieve his goal of reaching the Oasis.

17

Brio was a beautiful owl. His feathers were warm shades of brown and beige, and his elegant, intelligent eyes seemed to sparkle like jewels. His beak was strong and gracious, and Adir could only imagine how many words of wisdom he had uttered over the years.

Brio landed beside Adir and stretched his right leg and right wing behind him, then his left leg and wing. After briefly shaking his head, the wise owl settled into a comfortable position.

Adir stood still, somewhat stunned, and waited for Brio to say something.

After a lengthy silence, Brio looked at Adir with deep, penetrating eyes and repeated his question: "Indeed, Adir, what is your destiny?"

Frankly, Adir had been hoping for *answers*, not more questions. He scratched his head and shrugged all six of his shoulders.

"Err . . . well, for starters . . . I would like to say hello, Mr. Brio, sir. Um, I've heard a great deal about you. *And, dude!* Your reputation certainly precedes you! But, um, as for your question, well, I'm afraid I don't know the answer. I sure wish I did . . . In fact, now that you're here, I was kinda hoping *you* would tell *me*."

As owls are wont to do, Brio swiveled his head around in one swift circular motion—scaring the daylights out of Adir. *Yikes!* Adir thought to himself uncomfortably, *What a day I'm having!*

"Well," the owl said in his low voice, "perhaps if you're willing to listen, Adir, I may be able to help you find your destiny."

Needless to say, Adir was excited and curious all at once. He leaned forward expectantly and waited for Brio to continue.

"Adir," the owl said steadily, "you're a creature of great potential and intellect wrapped in a tiny package. And believe me when I tell you, you have a very special gift."

"I do?"

Brio looked down at the wide-eyed ant. "Yes, you do. In fact, most ants don't have a clue about this gift."

Adir was so intently curious he could hardly stand it. What was the gift? Why hadn't someone told him this earlier?

"Brio, sir . . . what's the gift?"

"The gift, Adir, is that you have the ability to communicate with elephants."

"I can speak to elephants?" asked Adir in disbelief.

"Yes, and there's something else I think you'll find a bit shocking."

"What is it?" asked Adir tentatively.

"Well, if you will crawl onto my claw, I will show you."

Adir was beyond asking questions. At this point, he was so stunned, so totally overwhelmed, he simply did as he was told. As quickly as he could, he scrambled onto Brio's claw, and before he knew it, he was sailing through the air. In a single, fluid movement, Brio took three short hops to the left, although for Adir it seemed like they had just traveled miles.

"Now, Adir," Brio said, "crawl off my claw and look around you."

Adir again did as he was told, but this time he couldn't believe his eyes. Adir stood on the ledge of a sloping cliff, but it wasn't any normal cliff. At a certain point, the land extended outward like a long, round extension of terrain, then disappeared. It was as though Adir were looking at the end of the world. His mind raced. *Was this where I landed that stormy night? The end of the world?*

"Mr. Brio, I don't know what's going on! This is really weird. Where am I?"

Brio could hear the fright in Adir's voice and quickly told him not to worry. "Adir, for your entire life you've lived on the back of an elephant. I've just transported you, however, to the elephant's head. What you're looking at is the slow curve of his trunk. Believe it or not, the storm that deposited you here actually moved you from one part of this enormous elephant's body to another."

Adir was in shock. He felt as if the ground had just dropped out from under him (though in reality, he should have felt as though the *elephant* had just dropped out from

19

under him). Nevertheless, his throat went dry, and he could swear he was beginning to lose his sight.

"I . . . I . . . I've been living on an *elephant's back* my whole life?" Adir paused and looked at the ground. "You mean, while I've been thinking and dreaming and planning, trying to figure out how to change things, I haven't actually been in control of where I'm going? Oh, I think I'm going to be sick. This is just too much. I've been riding on the back of an elephant this whole time? I really don't feel well. I can't feel my antennae. Do you mind if I sit down?"*

"Please do," the owl said, a touch concerned for the ant.

"Wait a minute," continued Adir with his head between his legs. "Do you mean to say that I might have thought I was heading west, and without knowing it, I was actually heading east?" Adir's questions faded into silence as he tried to process this unsettling news. He felt shock, disbelief, anger, nausea. Of course, they don't call Brio the "Wise Owl" for nothing; he had anticipated that Adir would feel all of this—and then some.

"Adir, I know this is hard to accept, but once you get used to it, you'll realize that what may seem like a disadvantage now is, in truth, an opportunity with huge potential. You're a special creature in the savannah, Adir. Your ability to talk to elephants puts you in an enviable position; because of this gift you have the potential to become a great leader. So many creatures and insects like you live on the backs of other animals and never even know it. Not only do you know it, but you can profit from it, as well. If you'd like, I'll teach you how to guide your elephant. With your exceptional will power and a well-guided elephant, you'll see that you can accomplish great things."

20

* You've probably picked up on this already, but Adir has some "melodramatic" tendencies.

"Do you mean that I could get to the Oasis one day?" asked Adir hopefully, finally coming up for air.

"That, and much more. The entire world is yours to discover, but you must realize that you and your elephant are inseparable. Think of it this way, Adir: you and your elephant are a team. You're the conscious element, and your elephant is the subconscious element. You're the thinking, critical side of this operation, and your elephant is the engine and vehicle that power your intellectual efforts. Though you are small and he is large, your influence over him is very powerful. Therefore, it is up to you to be mindful of the messages you give your elephant. You must learn to cooperate with him and work together to reach common goals."

"You mean my elephant wants to go to the Oasis, too?" Adir asked, shaking his little black head in disbelief.

"That's something you will have to find out. Think of your elephant as an extension of your inner self."

"Huh?"

"Let me put it another way. Alone, it would take you a very long time to achieve your goal of reaching the Oasis. Considering your size and how far away it is, it might even take you years. But if you can guide your elephant, the distance becomes much shorter. Remember, this elephant is *two million* times larger and more powerful than you. If you harness the power of your elephant, you will tap into a fountain of possibilities. In fact, if you can learn how to guide and lead your elephant, there is no telling what you will accomplish."

Adir still seemed a little confused, so Brio decided to give him an example. He asked Adir to look at the sky and tell him what he saw.

21

"I see blue sky. And I see the sun, which is way too bright," Adir said, covering his forehead with his left front foot. "I see clouds, big clouds. A few birds."

"What are the clouds doing?" Brio asked.

"Well, they're not producing rain. They're just sort of floating along."

"And how do they float along?"

"With the breeze, the wind. The wind pushes them across the sky."

"So, Adir, without the wind can the clouds move across the sky?"

"No, I guess they can't. You can have clouds, and you can have wind, but if you want the clouds to move, the wind has to *guide* the clouds."

"And so it is with your elephant," Brio said in his deep, reverberating voice. "Adir, from here on out, you need to accept that you and your elephant are in this together. You can be your elephant's guide, just like the wind. Eventually, you'll learn that he can be your guide as well."

Adir was in a bit of a daze. All these revelations were a lot to handle for a little ant.

"I still can't get over the fact that all this time I've been living on the back of an elephant," he muttered. But then another startling thought occurred to him. "Wait a minute! What does this elephant think about a tiny ant telling him what to do? And what's more, I don't know how I feel about having an elephant as my boss, either."

"Your elephant has powers you don't have, and you have gifts your elephant doesn't have. You shouldn't think of yourselves as two separate creatures. You are a team that can either work together or act independently. Your mission— should you choose to accept it—is to harness the power of your elephant to reach the Oasis. The choice is all yours."

Adir swore he could hear a familiar theme song pipe in. He had to admit to himself that he was prepared to do just about anything* if it meant getting to the Oasis.

"Oh, there is one other thing I should tell you," Brio said. "You can communicate with your elephant, but your elephant can't talk to you."

"What? He can't speak?" whined Adir. "Then how am I going to tell him what to do?"

"Adir, you're not going to be giving Elgo orders and telling him what to do. You're going to be guiding him, inspiring him, *motivating* him. You need to support and empower him."

"Is that his name?" Adir scoffed, "Elgo?"

Brio nodded, and Adir could detect an amused twinkle in the old owl's eye.

Adir put his head in his hands. "This is all so confusing," he cried. "One minute I'm with my colony, and the next, I'm all alone. And now, to make things even more baffling, I find out I've been living on an elephant my whole entire . . . *Wait one leaf-cutting minute!* Why can't I just up and leave and go back to my colony?"

Brio's eyes sparkled. "That's a good question. Unfortunately, I can't tell you the answer. I can only tell you that should you set out to find your colony now, you will not find the Oasis. Furthermore, you will not master the lessons of The Ant and the Elephant, and unfortunately, that means you won't become the leader you've always dreamed of becoming. Before any creature can become a great leader to others, he must first understand himself. Once he knows how to ignite his own vision and take the steps needed to achieve his own goals, he can empower and motivate others to join him."

23

---

* Telemarketing. Acting in infomercials. Acting in infomercials about telemarketing.

Before you can become a great leader to others, you first must understand yourself.

Brio could tell that his words were making a lot of sense to Adir. The owl continued: "By returning to your colony now, Adir, you'll be retreating to your old familiar ways, but if this is what you want to do, I'll point you in the right direction. It'll take you some time to get there, but you can certainly make it. However," Brio paused, "if you decide to work with your elephant and learn how to communicate and listen to your 'inner self,' then you'll be able to find the Oasis and be reunited with your colony, as well. Perhaps more importantly, after having learned how to guide the elephant-sized subconscious that stands beneath you, you'll be in a position to become the most effective leader you can be. Your first step is to determine which of these options excites and inspires you, Adir. You must choose which path you want to follow and commit to it; otherwise, nothing good will come of either choice. It's up to you, Adir."

Adir was faced with a choice that confronts many of us: he could go back to life as he knew it, or he could courageously take on a new challenge. The little ant weighed these options carefully.

If he returned to his colony now, he would be accepting a well-known, yet disappointing and stressful existence. He couldn't deny the truth: he was missing something at work, and this affected his proficiency as a leader. If he went back now, he would continue to worry about what the Queen thought of his performance, and every day would be fraught with anxiety about his competence and frustration about his deficiency.

Or he could venture into the unknown and *discover* his potential. Heck! Maybe he would even discover his destiny. Maybe this adventure would teach him something about himself. Maybe, he thought, feeling that tingle again, he would learn how to be a better leader. If he could find the Oasis, surely he would be able to find his colony, too.

It didn't take him long to make up his mind. He snapped to attention and saluted the wise owl.

"Brio, sir, I am ready to get to work!"

4

The Journey Worth Taking

Brio looked long and hard at Adir. "Are you ready to begin your lesson, Adir?" Adir could sense that the owl was sizing him up. He leaned forward and nodded, ready to learn whatever Brio would teach him. *How wonderful it would be to finally find the way to the Oasis,* he thought to himself.

Brio cleared his throat and began. "Adir, I will now describe to you exactly how to get to the Oasis."

Adir burst in, "Is it *west*? It is, isn't it? I knew it!"

Brio rotated his head from one side to the other. "No, Adir, it requires more than simply knowing which direction to travel. To get to the Oasis, you must first learn how to guide and direct your elephant—how to cooperate with him and move him in the same direction you're traveling. This may be easier said than done, however."

"Oh," said Adir, somewhat deflated, "how do I do that?"

"You speak his language, Adir. The language of the elephant is defined by how you respond to the challenges and successes you encounter during your journey. Elgo will listen to and remember everything you say and think, except . . . "

"Except what?"

"Except that those stubborn elephants have minds of their own, and they have incredible memories. This memory includes some bad habits—patterns, really—and a somewhat shaky confidence level," said Brio.

"Really?" Adir was beginning to wonder what he had gotten himself into. This was just like back at the colony; his delegation of ants never wanted to change their ways.

Brio could sense that Adir was worried again, so he continued. "Elephants do not question things. They have a that's-just-the-way-it-is mentality. If you suggest something an elephant thinks is risky or impractical, he will continue with the status quo. It's in the elephant's nature to always do what he's been taught, to always repeat what he's done before."

"Instinct, right? But isn't that a good thing? What if Elgo is protecting us?" asked Adir. "What if he does that because he senses something dangerous?"

"Yes, Adir, your elephant will protect you from harm. But he may also, out of instinct, try to protect you from situations that scare him. In reality, these situations could be opportunities to grow. Make fear your friend, not your master; fear can be a powerful motivator if you learn to manage it."

Adir found a little twig and a leaf to take notes.* He decided this was a good tip to write down: **Make fear your friend, not your master**. He repeated the phrase to himself as he wrote it down. *What do you know?* he thought to himself. *This is just like my delegation of ants. They were always steering clear of change, and I could never figure out why, but this makes total sense; they were afraid of change!*

---

* That's right. The twig writes. Deal with it.

But then Adir started to think about himself. He scratched his head with his right antenna. He searched for words as he reviewed his own life, looking back over all the things he had dreamed about doing but had never achieved. He had to admit to himself that he found leadership a stressful prospect. He was frequently afraid of failure, and because of that, he hesitated to lead with *confidence*. This new information amazed Adir. Throughout his life he had wanted to change his destiny but had never known how. He was beginning to realize Brio was right—he needed to be a leader to himself before he could lead others.

"Now, Adir, it's important to know why you shouldn't let fear be your master," Brio said.

"Ah, yes. Good point, sir!" Adir put down his twig and leaf and gazed intently at the owl. "Why is that?"

"Well, it's quite clear, isn't it? You don't know what you don't know," said Brio. "This is a very useful notion. *You don't know what you don't know.* For example, only an hour ago, you didn't know that you were riding on the back of an elephant. You didn't know that for every step you took in one direction, Elgo actually could've been walking in another," said Brio. "You must open your mind to discover possibilities that might not seem obvious to you at the time."

"So true, so true!" Adir picked up his stick and leaf and made another note to himself, directly under the previous one. **You don't know what you don't know. Open your mind to discover possibilities that might not seem obvious at the time.**

"So," Brio said, "let's find out what you don't know about yourself. Let's find out what's at the core of your being, Adir. What's inside that teeny little body of yours? What's most important to you? What have you got in that miniature heart?"

29

"Well . . . " Adir said, feeling slightly smaller than usual, "*that* doesn't sound so hard. Let me think about it for a second. Oh, I remember! Getting to the Oasis—*duh!*" Adir shot his fist into the air with enthusiasm.

"It might seem like a simple question, Adir, but you've got to take 'what is most important to you' to the furthest point possible. To discover this, you simply need to ask yourself one question: *Why?*"

"That's funny. Since you're an owl, I thought your question would be *who!*" said Adir with a playful smile.*

Brio failed to see the humor. "Are you done?"

"Yes. Sorry, sir," said Adir.

"Good." Brio continued, "When you can't ask yourself *why* any further, then you know you've reached what I call the *core*. Adir, think of a coconut. If you were to see it cut in half, you'd see a number of layers. The tough, fibrous weave is a difficult exterior to break through. Then there's the hard layer that must be cracked. Then there's the meaty layer. Finally, the core of the coconut holds a sweet, milky treasure. Each layer seems to protect an inner layer. Your core is just like the coconut's core, and to get to the treasures inside you, you need to ask yourself *why*."

"But, Brio, I know my goal; I want to get to the Oasis. So how come I need to know my core, too?"

"Good question, little ant. The core is what motivates you. It's the answer to the question, 'What makes you feel alive?'" said the wise owl, ruffling his feathers with a delicious shiver. "I want you to think about what you love to do most. Then ask yourself why you love it."

"But how will this help me get to the Oasis?" Adir asked.

"Adir, before you start any journey, you must know why the journey is worth the effort it will take to get you there. Your core—the answer to your *why*—will remain constant

---

* Ant humor is of the "Boy Scout" variety.

throughout your life. It is essential to your happiness, to finding the Oasis and to achieving any other goal you set for yourself. Your *why* will keep you moving forward even when your elephant wants to head in the opposite direction. Your *why* will keep you headed toward the Oasis even when you are exhausted, distressed and anxious. Your *why* will keep your goal in focus and your vision clear, even when other ants tell you the goal is not such a big deal. In fact, your *why* is almost as important as the Oasis itself—you can't get there without this vital step."

"Sounds like a pretty powerful concept," Adir said, noting it to himself. ***Clarify your vision. Zero in on a goal that has a depth of meaning. The journey has to be worth taking.***

"Okay, Brio, I believe you," said Adir, "and when I'm sure of my *why,* I know *who—who* to call!"

This time, Brio opened his beak in a slight smile and rolled his eyes. "You just won't quit, will you?" He bowed his body to one side, extended his great wings and flew away.

31

Adir's Notes to Self

Clarify your vision.

- Make fear your friend, not your master.

- You don't know what you don't know. Open your mind to discover possibilities that may not be obvious at the time.

- Zero in on a goal that has a depth of meaning. The journey has to be worth taking.

Waking Up to Awareness

It had been three days and nights since Brio revealed to Adir that he was living on top of Elgo's back. The days were blistering hot and the nights were cool and breezy. From what Adir could tell from his perch atop Elgo's head, they were headed somewhere, although he wasn't sure where. He wondered whether Elgo knew where he was marching. If only he could ask the elephant and the elephant could tell him. What a challenge this was proving to be!

He was still trying to master Brio's first lesson, and this, too, was proving harder than he could ever have anticipated. Over and over he asked himself, *Why do I want to get to the Oasis? Why is this goal important to me? What is at my core? Do I have a core? Brio says I have a core—so I guess I have a core . . . but what is my core . . .?**

Adir tried to concentrate on Elgo, as well, and what was going through the big elephant's mind. He even pressed his tiny ear to Elgo's head to see if he could hear anything.

---

* Ever notice that when you say certain words over and over, they start to sound weird? Core, core, core, core, core, core, core, core, core, core . . .

Sometimes he sensed nothing; it was as though the monotony of this long march through the hot terrain had fried Elgo's brain. It was as though they were just trudging along, day in and day out.

Like many creatures in the savannah, elephants naturally gravitate toward feelings of pleasure and bliss. For Elgo, this meant lying down in a mud hole on a hot, dry day, his stomach full of fresh greens and his herd nearby. Unfortunately, there was a drought that year, so there was no mud or greens around. As for his herd, Elgo had no idea where it was. Times were tough for everyone. The herd had separated because they couldn't seem to find enough food for everyone, and this caused a great deal of consternation among the elephants. They had decided that everyone might be better off on his own.

Still, as Adir and Elgo marched on, Elgo let his mind drift to those things that made him happiest, even though he knew it was unlikely he would find them. The very thought of these things—the gooey, cool mud on his legs, the bitter taste of freshly picked greens and the camaraderie of his fellow elephants—made him smile a big elephant-sized grin. He swung his trunk from side to side and flapped his floppy ears. He loved the slight breeze that his big ears and trunk made on his front legs. All sorts of happy thoughts floated through Elgo's mind.

While Elgo was daydreaming, Adir became aware of a deep buzz resonating from the ground below his feet. He pressed his ear to the elephant's body and realized that Elgo was humming! Adir could feel the vibrations of the elephant's vocal chords through Elgo's thick skin. He could not only could he hear the tune, but he could also feel it through his entire body. What a lovely sensation it was! Adir stretched out flat on his back and let the buzzing massage his body. Adir even began to hum along with the elephant, although given his almost microscopic size in comparison to the elephant, Adir's hum was a few octaves higher.

Lying on his back, Adir closed his eyes and instantly pictured Elgo lying in a cool mud hole. In his mind's eye he could see the happy elephant swaying his massive head from side to side. Adir smiled at the thought. Since learning about his elephant from Brio, a whole new world had opened up to him. He was now aware of sounds, feelings and thoughts that he had never noticed before.

But then something happened. The humming stopped. All of a sudden the image of horrible, dangerous teeth came into Adir's mind. He quickly scrambled to his feet and looked to see what was happening. A guttural shriek came from Elgo, and out from behind two thick bushes jumped a lion and a lioness. There was no doubt about it—these animals were desperate for food and willing to fight for it. Elgo had no intention of being another animal's dinner, though. He reacted instantly and instinctually, letting loose yet another guttural shriek—and this one was so loud it carried across the savannah.

The lions snarled and readied themselves for an attack. Adir was terrified! He buried his head under his legs and prayed for the best.

To his surprise, Elgo began to charge the lions. Dirt and debris flew in all directions as the ten-ton animal rushed his attackers. The speed of the elephant stirred a wind that literally pinned Adir's antennae to the top of his head. Elgo's tusks proved to be such fearsome weapons that the lions didn't quite know what to do. In less than a heartbeat, the lions' offense turned to a defense, and they scrambled for cover.

35

Adir popped up on top of Elgo's head and took in the show. He never realized how fast Elgo could move, but then, he'd only just discovered that Elgo existed!

Adir stood up on his two hind legs. "Scaredy cats!" Adir called. "King of the jungle? *Ha!* We'll show you who rules the savannah!" Then Adir began twisting his hips to the right, his shoulders to the left and vice versa. Elgo could sense that Adir was dancing and readily joined in, swinging his trunk, flapping his gigantic ears and stomping his feet. He wiggled his enormous behind and jiggled his massive girth. If you've never seen an elephant do the twist, trust me—it is a sight to behold.*

But then, mid-twist, Elgo stopped and peered into a stand of trees. Leaning over and squinting, he took a closer look. Before Adir knew what had happened, Elgo was quickly retreating in the direction from which they had just come.

This time, Elgo's shriek was high-pitched and panicky. As Elgo stumbled backward, Adir tumbled head over heels. When the tiny ant finally caught his footing, he looked back to see what had frightened Elgo so.

Between the clouds of dust and the stand of trees, Adir saw something that made no sense whatsoever to him. Apparently, Elgo had heard the distinctive and unmistakable sound of mice—not just one mouse, but a whole nest. There, behind them, was a group of arrogant mice waving their fists at the frightened elephant.

"Why, those little . . . " Adir said to himself when he realized that some of the mice were blowing raspberries at them.

He crawled back to the top of Elgo's head and peered over the side to speak to the elephant.

"Are you kidding me? You just chased not one, but two lions away, and now you're afraid of mice? You're totally

* Think Richard Simmons . . . only bigger . . . and *sans* the offensive spandex.

irrational, Elgo! It's as though you don't even think about things, but just react to them! What is it with you?"

Adir was in shock. He couldn't believe that in one instant, the elephant would fight to protect himself, and in the next he was high-tailing off in the other direction like a lily-livered coward—over mice, of all things!

"This is ridiculous!" he cried, throwing his legs up to the sky.

Adir spread his body across Elgo's bumpy hide and began to concentrate intently. This was as good a time as any to see if he really could communicate with the elephant. He thought soothing thoughts and spoke calmly, "Relax, breathe deeply." It didn't take long for Adir to sense that Elgo was beginning to do just that.

• • •

37

That night, Adir thought about what had happened. It reminded him of a time back at the colony when the sight of a snake hanging in a nearby tree had sent his delegation of ants into a frenzy. They had scurried around and hidden for the rest of the day, and even after the snake had long since slithered away, Adir couldn't get his team to come out and get back to work. *Fear is like quick sand,* he thought to himself. *Once you step in it, it will just pull you down.*

Adir realized other similarities between his connection to Elgo and his connection to his workforce. He needed his team to work hard so the Queen would be pleased with his delegation's performance, just as he needed Elgo to march in the direction of the Oasis. Of course there's a flip side to that leaf. Adir needed to figure out a way to get his workforce on track in order to achieve their goals, just like he now had to find a way to get Elgo on track and head in the right direction.

Adir realized that if they were going to get to the Oasis, his and Elgo's goals had to be in alignment.

6

Harnessing the Power of Emotions

The next day, the sun rose over the horizon like a big, fiery ball in the eastern sky. The activity throughout the savannah was as obvious to the ears as it was to the eyes. In the distant trees the sound of birds fell into two categories: one flock of birds chirped in delight as another flock squawked in seeming disdain for anything that moved. Cicadas filled the air with waves of whirring, white noise. Small, furry animals scurried for cover, knowing full well that menacing talons were poised high above in the thermal currents.

Adir was foraging for food when he heard the sound of wings overhead and soon found Brio next to him on Elgo's back. Adir welcomed the wise owl's return, and they settled in for the next lesson.

"There are five action steps that I will ask you to incorporate into your life over the next few weeks, Adir. These action steps are tools to help you reach your goals . . . your *Oasis*, if you will."

"I'm ready, Brio," said Adir emphatically with his twig and leaf in hand. "Tell me what the five action steps are."

"All in good time, my little friend," replied Brio, lifting his wings and fluttering slightly. "First, I want to discuss something else."

"Sure, fire away," Adir replied.

"Remember, Adir, when we discussed the coconut and the layers surrounding the core?"

"Yes," answered Adir, proud to be able to keep up with Brio's train of thought. "You told me to find out what's at the core of my being."

"That's right, Adir. Now, when last we spoke, you had identified getting to the Oasis as your goal, but remember how we talked about searching for the *why*?"

"Oh, yes, of course I do!" replied Adir. He had been searching for his *why* for days now.

"Getting to the Oasis is your goal—but *why*, Adir? Have you figured out why that is so important to you?"

Adir took a deep breath. "I have indeed thought about it, Brio. The reason I want to get to the Oasis is this: I'll be able to live a perfect life there. I won't have to search for food and water. I won't have to worry about lions and windstorms and crawling under Elgo's ear to get out of the hot sun. In fact, in the Oasis, my life will pretty much be perfect."

"*Why?*"

"Because I won't have to spend all my time struggling so hard to survive. I'll be able to do other things that really matter. So, living in the Oasis is the most important thing to me."

"*Why?*" Brio prodded gently.

"Because in the Oasis, I'll be free to think about other things. I won't have to worry about just getting by—I'll have the freedom to be curious."*

---

* Single black ant seeks enlightenment, food, Oasis-like environment, leadership skills for life of frolic and self-actualization. No food-stashers, please.

"And . . ."

"And I'll be reunited with my colony, and I'll be able to be a better leader to my delegation because I now know how important that is to me."

"And . . ."

"And when I'm free to live and not just survive, and when I'm the best leader for my fellow ants as I can be—well, I'll be the happiest ant in the whole world!"

Brio paused to let Adir take in what he had just said.

"Well, Adir, it seems to me you've identified three core experiences: the freedom to be curious, becoming a leader your fellow ants will want to follow and living a life of bliss," said Brio.

Adir smiled. "Okay, so how do I make this happen? Let's get the show on the road! Tell me the tools, oh, Wise Winged One."

Brio's eyes sparkled at Adir's good-natured impertinence,* but he played the straight man nonetheless. "Adir, get your twig and leaf ready, because I'm going to tell you your first action step. You need to find the *elephant buzz*," Brio said, knowing that he would have to explain further. "Adir, we must never underestimate the power of emotions in our lives. By tapping into your emotions, you'll discover what motivates you. Your passions will ignite your vision. Emotions run deep—past your amazing ant intellect and far into your elephant's brain—for what you feel, Elgo feels as well. You can inspire your elephant by tapping into the power of your emotions."

Adir was a little puzzled, but he wrote down the information all the same. ***ACTION STEP #1: Find the elephant buzz. Find the emotion that ignites the vision. Inspire your team through emotion. <u>Never underestimate the power of emotion.</u>***

41

---

* Impertinence affects everyone. See a doctor.

Adir looked at what he had written and thought for a minute. He understood what Brio meant by the emotion stuff, but what the heck was an *elephant buzz*? He looked at the owl with narrowed eyes, *"What you talking about, Brio?"*

"I know it sounds a little funny, but let's try to understand this together. Adir, I want you to tell me more about what it would be like for you to live in a place or a situation where your three core experiences are met. What would it be like to have the freedom to be curious, to be a leader worth following and to live the life you've always wanted in a state of bliss?"

"I would have to describe the Oasis," Adir said with conviction, "because to me, the Oasis is a place that is vibrant and full of life. It's a place where there's plenty of food and tons of stuff to explore. In the Oasis, there are other ant colonies where perhaps I'll help teach the lessons of The Ant and the Elephant—all of the things you're teaching me. There's abundance in the Oasis. I have no doubt about it: that's the place to find bliss."

"Great!" said Brio. "Now, describe to me the important details you would *experience* in the Oasis. Make sure you include all five senses in your description."

Adir closed his eyes and thought very hard. He imagined the whole circle of life vibrating with energy. Beautiful, sunny days washed over the teeming collection of animals, plants and insects. Rain fed the lush green trees and grass. The rippling lake reflected the clouds and mirrored the birds frolicking in the sky. Beneath the surface of the cool, fresh water, fish darted between the legs of lounging hippos and among the swaying bulrushes. Birds warbled from the trees while frogs and crickets kept the beat on the forest floor. The sunshine filtered in through the tropical canopy.

"Let's see," began Adir, trying to put his beautiful vision into language, "I'm standing in the middle of all my ant friends—friends I haven't seen in so long and whom I miss so much. We're celebrating my first anniversary of coming to the Oasis. I *see* the colors surrounding us are the greens of nature, the blue sky and the gray skin of my elephant, Elgo. I *hear* the sound of a waterfall in the distance, along with the sound of a slight breeze rustling the large palm leaves overhead. I *smell* honeysuckle, coconut trees and the food we've laid out for the feast. I *taste* those delicious treats we've worked so hard to prepare. I *feel* the shaking and rubbing of my antennae with other ants as we all dance." Adir opened one eye. "How's that?"

"Not bad," Brio said with the pleased expression of a sage professor, "but now I want you to imagine the feelings you would have there. Experience the feelings as if you were there right now."

43

Adir closed his eyes again and concentrated harder than he ever knew he could. The images of the Oasis came to him like waves washing over his body.

"The feeling is total satisfaction," he said aloud with his eyes still closed. He imagined his team sitting together on a log after a long, hard day of rewarding work. They were laughing and telling stories and thinking about how they could do things better the following day. They were excited to be part of Adir's team.

"I feel connected to my fellow ants!" he said, beginning to stand up. "I'm proud of my team, and I'm proud of myself! My team is even proud of *me*!"

A feeling started to fill his little body. It bubbled from his legs all the way up to his head like a rising thermometer. He opened his eyes and shouted with glee, "I feel alive, Brio! I feel *alive*!"

Suddenly, the massive elephant underneath Adir's body shuddered and sent the starry-eyed Adir stumbling backward.

"What was that?" he squeaked.

"That was exactly what you want to happen, Adir," said Brio excitedly. "You just experienced the *elephant buzz*. This reaction from your elephant is precisely what I've been talking about. You and Elgo are connected in a special way. What you *think* is communicated to your elephant. Believe it or not, Adir, you can be a good leader to Elgo if you keep those feelings in your mind as often as possible."

"You mean that every time I think about how I'd feel living in the Oasis, Elgo will think and feel it, too?"

"Just about. And here's the most important part: if your thoughts and dreams match up with something important to your elephant, then there will be a reaction."

"What do you mean by that, Brio?"

"Well, if you and Elgo have the same goals, and you feel the same way about achieving them, then you'll be aligned. Your goals—and feelings about those goals—will have a powerful effect on your teamwork."

Brio continued, "Adir, it's good to remember that Elgo's mind is roughly two million times larger than your mind, and, Adir, your mind is incredibly intelligent. This means that the wisdom hidden in your elephant's mind is vast. The challenge is to find what the wisdom is. The *elephant buzz* is an effective tool you can use to gauge when your ideas match up with Elgo's dreams. When you visualize an idea and communicate it to Elgo, you may be able to get that telltale sign of a shuddering elephant; the mind and body are connected. If you feel that buzz up and down your spine, pay attention. Pay careful attention to whatever energizes your elephant. Then, identify what made him excited. The *elephant buzz* is an I'm-in-the-right-place sort of feeling. Once you learn to recognize the *elephant buzz*, you'll know that you're communicating with your partner in an effective way. You'll be tapping into Elgo's own vision of a perfect life, and by doing that, you'll inspire and motivate him."

"Remember," Brio cautioned, "it's important to practice this harmonious alignment between you and Elgo during quiet times when there are no distractions. This is what I call 'experiencing your vision.' Imagining your future goals in such a setting will quickly give you a sense of anticipation or anxiety, perhaps both. If you're anxious, ask yourself why. Why would you feel anxiety? What would be the consequences in your life if you pursued your goal? More importantly, what price would you pay if you didn't pursue something that gave you an *elephant buzz*? Would you feel regret? Would you be satisfied living with these regrets?"

Adir underlined the statement: ***Never underestimate the power of emotions.*** He put down his twig and thought.

45

"Wow!" exclaimed Adir. "You know, Brio, the other day I really felt like I was communicating with Elgo. I was daydreaming about something and felt the ground—I mean the elephant—underneath me start to hum, and well, it was the first time I felt like Elgo and I were really connecting. And now—let me make sure I've got this right—you're saying that I should not only have a conversation with my elephant, but I should also pay attention to the response I get from Elgo. I should *listen* to him."

"Every chance you get, Adir, you should *experience your vision* and see how your elephant responds. This way, Elgo will lock your vision into his amazing memory."

"So all I have to do is have an imagined experience and my elephant will get the buzz?" asked Adir.

"Yes, but there are exceptions," said Brio. "For instance, you could try to force a vision on Elgo that may mean a great deal to you, but very little to him. As a result, you won't get any *elephant buzz* whatsoever."

"Huh?" grunted Adir as he swiveled his head to the side and crossed his eyes for effect.

Brio, ignoring the ant's overly dramatic expressions, responded, "My little friend, this has been a lot to absorb. There's still much to learn, but you'll have to wait for the next lesson. I have some business to attend to on the other side of the savannah. There are some squirrels and birds who haven't learned how to share the same tree just yet, and I think I can help."

"Well, what should I do now?" Adir asked.

"While I'm gone, I want you to refine your *elephant buzz*. I want you to tune in to your elephant and start to feel what he's feeling. I want you to get in touch with your intuition and experience your vision. Home in on what feels right for you. Imagine all five senses and the feelings of satisfaction that come with your vision of life in the Oasis, and then pay attention to Elgo's response. Is he on board with your vision? Does he want to live in the Oasis, too? Ask yourself *why* your vision should be important to Elgo."

With that, Brio flew away. He soared high above the treetops as his powerful wings caught a thermal updraft. Adir watched as his feathered friend spiraled up and up until he was a tiny, ant-like speck in the vast sky.

Adir's Notes to Self

Clarify your vision.

- Make fear your friend, not your master.

- You don't know what you don't know. Open your mind to discover possibilities that may not be obvious at the time.

- Zero in on a goal that has a depth of meaning. The journey has to be worth taking.

  ACTION STEP #1: Find the *elephant buzz*. Find the emotion that ignites the vision. Inspire your team through emotion. ***Never underestimate the power of emotion.***

7

Creating Positive Dominant Thoughts

Adir was excited about his newfound strategy of making Elgo shudder with anticipation as they focused on the same vision together, but he couldn't shake the feeling that the big elephant was still headed in the wrong direction. In fact, Adir was certain Elgo was going the wrong way, and this was a constant source of frustration and anxiety for the ant. That stressed-out throbbing sensation returned with even more intensity than before. Adir wasn't even this jittery back at the colony! What was going on? Why couldn't he get Elgo to do what he wanted him to do?

Adir tried to keep reminding himself of his vision as Brio had advised him to do, but he kept slipping back into his old habits. More often than not, he found himself sinking into the familiar feeling of frustration. Time and again, Adir had to shake off feelings of negativity and focus his mind in an attempt to recapture the *elephant buzz*. If and when the sensation did occur, it began to feel less and less exhilarating.

Before long, Adir was aggravated, frustrated and disillusioned with the many new ideas Brio had suggested to him. Negative thoughts, increasing in intensity and effect, built momentum and rushed through his mind like a mudslide down a mountain. He even began to take his frustrations out on poor Elgo.*

"Fine, Elgo," Adir complained. "If you want to go the wrong way for the rest of your life, then so be it! I'm just one ant and you're a big, lumbering elephant. Who am I to tell you what to do, right? Just wake me up when we get there . . . *wherever that is!*"

Of course, this negativity did not affect only the ant. Elgo was feeling waves of frustration, too. And since emotions are powerful influences on elephants, he began to feel blue more often than not. Elgo remembered all the other tough times he experienced in the past. He pictured the time when he had to leave his parents and go off on his own, and he thought about how he felt when the herd separated. He recalled the sad looks on the faces of the other elephants as he trudged off to find his own path. Elgo remembered realizing that he might never see any of them again. He pictured himself turning to take one last look and clearly remembered that the expressions on their faces said it all. Recalling these sad events caused tears to well up in Elgo's eyes, and he sniffled. This was not just an ordinary sniffle—what with a long trunk and all, this was a sniffle that reverberated through his entire body and could be heard for miles.

When Adir became discouraged, he would usually try his best to get back on track and recapture the *elephant buzz*, but at other times he would become overwhelmed with negative thoughts. *This whole Oasis thing is B.S.! I'm not meant*

* Like with mean jokes . . . *Hey, Lumpy. Knock, knock. Who's there? Elgo. Elgo who? Elgo nuts if you walk any slower, stupid elephant.*

*to get to the Oasis, and I'm certainly not meant to be a leader.
I'm just a tiny, insignificant ant at the mercy of a big, stupid
elephant. I might as well accept it; I'm not going to see my
colony anytime soon. Why did I sign up for this crazy adventure, anyway? If only I had chosen the path I'm accustomed
to and returned to my colony when I had the chance!*

It got so bad that one day he didn't even want to get up
in the morning. Fortunately, Brio appeared in the early
morning light. The still air made Brio work a little harder as
he flapped his expansive wings toward the elephant path.
He wasn't surprised to see that he had to backtrack in order
to locate Elgo and Adir. As he had suspected, Adir was
finding this action step difficult to master.

Finally, Brio came across Elgo's massive frame standing
like a statue on the path. The elephant seemed to be waiting
for something; it was as though he were stuck in a
daydream, staring off into the distance with a gaze fixed on
nothing in particular. *This*, Brio thought to himself, *is not
an inspired elephant.*

51

Brio landed gracefully on Elgo's back and immediately
looked around for Adir. The tiny ant was just beside one of
Elgo's ears, tossing and turning under a leaf. As it was long
after most ants had started their day of scurrying and
hurrying for sustenance, Brio knew he was in for a tough
day of tutelage.

"Adir," said Brio matter-of-factly, "let's get to work."

"What?" came an irritated voice from under the leaf.
"You want me to get to work? What's the use?"

"How's that *elephant buzz* coming along?" Brio asked
cautiously.

"Aw, come on, don't you have some mouse to scare or
something?" the muffled voice asked peevishly. "The *elephant*

buzz doesn't work, Brio. It's a load of rotten mangos, and you know it! I should've gone back to my colony when I had the chance. Now I'll never see them again!"

"Adir," said Brio in a strong and measured way, "I know that the last few days have been frustrating for you. I knew before I left you that they would be frustrating . . ."

Adir remained silent, utterly livid with Brio; it seemed to him as though the owl had given him false hope.

"Adir, let's give the Oasis another shot. I know how to fix your present state of frustration."

The leaf rustled, and Adir's antennae emerged from underneath it. He peeked his head out and said sarcastically, "Yeah? How's that?"

"Adir, my friend, if you come out from under your cover, I will tell you."

"You will?" Adir asked, still hidden. "And you promise it'll work?"

"Yes, Adir," Brio sighed. Even though he had known that Adir would experience frustration while trying to master the last lesson, he couldn't help but think that the ant was overdoing it a little. He checked the sun's position in the sky. He would be there all day if they didn't get started.

"Oh, all right," said Adir, emerging. "I'm here now. What do you have for me? How can I fix this?"

Brio paused to consider his words. "Well, Adir, first I want you to know that it was essential for you to struggle with this inner conflict. Without conflict there is no growth, and truthfully, the most challenging conflict is within ourselves. Resolving inner conflict empowers us to change our lives. Unfortunately, it's easier for us to diagnose problems in other creatures than it is to diagnose the problems in ourselves. To look within ourselves objectively is nearly impossible without some help from the outside. What you went through was difficult, but in order to grow, you must understand that this process is not an easy one. In order for you to fully understand the next lesson, I needed to let you struggle with the process. Now you know where some of the pitfalls are, and you can learn to navigate your way around them; you can truly implement change."

Without conflict there is no growth, and the most challenging conflict is within ourselves.

53

Adir looked at Brio for a few seconds and then skeptically asked, "How?"

"Adir, today I'll share another concept and action step with you, but first, let me ask you a question. You've wanted to get to the Oasis for a long time, right?"

"Since that crow ate all my food, I have!"

"Yet the results aren't keeping pace with the efforts you're putting forth. Why do you think that is?"

"It's Elgo's fault. He's the one who has been going in the wrong direction. I *try* to communicate with him, but clearly this big ol' pachyderm isn't *interested* in listening. Every morning I wake up ready to work toward the Oasis, just like you said, and still he just lumbers along, munching on grass, looking for mud . . . all the usual 'elephant' stuff. It's just like back at the colony—my team never *really* listened to me;

they just did what they always did. They may have said they *could* change, but they weren't *willing* to do anything differently. And now, with this big lug of an elephant, what chance do I have? After all, I'm just a tiny ant! My elephant has two million times the power that I have—you even said so! How am I supposed to move him?"

"Oooooh, you're on to something," said Brio. "When you say two million times the power, what do you mean?"

Adir cocked his head. That wasn't the response he expected from Brio. He thought the owl would admonish him for complaining so much.

"Well," he began, "Elgo seems to be the one in control of where we go. It's as if he decides even when I'm trying to tell him otherwise," the ant said stubbornly, crossing four of his legs.

"In a way, this is true. Your elephant and you are inextricably connected in thought and action, yet you think one thing and your elephant thinks another," Brio replied. "I know something about elephants, Adir, and your elephant in particular. You see, elephants survive because they follow their instincts, what they learn from their parents and other experiences in their lives. Because they eventually have to fend for themselves, they learn to follow a certain path without question—a path that has kept generations of elephants safe from harm. But I know for a fact that elephants long for the Oasis just as ants do . . . as all creatures do, actually. The dilemma is that your elephant's reality is different from yours."

"What do you mean, *his reality*? Correct me if I'm wrong, oh, Kung Fu Master—I mean Brio—but I was under the distinct impression that Elgo and I are in the same place here."

"If you had to name them, what would Elgo's beliefs, attitudes and truths be in regard to the possibility of reaching the Oasis?" asked Brio.

"Beliefs, attitudes and truths?"

"Yes."

"Well, seeing as how we're not getting results, I would say that the big fella doesn't *believe* the Oasis exists. His *attitude* would be not to expect it, and his *truth*—if you want to call it that—would be that it ain't gonna happen," responded Adir a little too flippantly.

"And the solution would be?" asked Brio.

"The solution would be to shift Elgo's beliefs, attitudes and truths, to make him believe he should relocate to a piece of real estate in the middle of the Oasis," replied the ant, stomping one of his feet. "But what about the frustration I experienced these past few weeks? What about *my* stress level?! I didn't seem to have any impact on Elgo when thinking about my vision of the Oasis and trying to generate an *elephant buzz*. Frankly, I got bupkis!"*

"How many times did you try to get your elephant to pay attention to your vision of the future in the Oasis?" asked the owl.

"Tons!"

"Really? How many times is tons?"

"A couple of . . . er . . . ah . . . hmmmm—maybe a *dozen*?" said Adir as he realized Brio was about to embark on another lesson.

"And therein lies the problem—a problem that can be solved if you understand the concept I'm about to share with you. I call this concept *Drops in the Bucket*."

Adir took out the twig and leaf again and readied himself to be enlightened.

"Imagine, Adir, that you have a bucket full of clear, fresh water. Now imagine that your goal in life is to turn the water in the bucket a brilliant blue."

55

* Which is a Yiddish word for "nada," which is a Spanish word for "diddly," which is a Dot Commer's word for "R.O.I."

"What kind of a goal is it to have a bucket of blue water?" asked Adir, wondering if his teacher had taken a wrong turn into a tall tree.

"It's a concept that will help you understand why you became so frustrated over the last few weeks," responded Brio in a monotone. "Adir, sometimes we need to trust that we're getting closer to our goal, even though we see no proof of any progress."

"Okay, I'll play along. I've *always* wanted a blue bucket," said Adir as he gave a wink and shrugged a couple of right shoulders.

"Now, Adir, imagine that you have a bucket that will hold five thousand gallons of water. In your efforts to turn the bucket of water blue, you must follow one rule: you cannot put more than one drop of blue dye in the bucket each day. So if you miss a day, you can't catch up the next day with more than one drop."

Adir was beginning to see the relevance of this concept. He stopped being such a wisenheimer and really began to listen.

"If you're excited about the prospect of getting a bucket of blue water," Brio continued, "you'll probably have an *elephant buzz* every time you think about it, right? But what happens that first day when you take your eyedropper and put one drop of blue dye in a five-thousand-gallon bucket?"

"Not much, I suppose. It's just one drop, after all," responded Adir.

"Yes, but you tell yourself you've just started. You're still excited, optimistic and hopeful. So the next day and the next and the next, you plop the dye in the bucket only to see it dissipate and disappear. Despite the fact that there's the tiniest blue tinge in the bucket, you don't see it because you see the bucket every day, and the change is gradual."

Adir wrote down the action step, although he was still a little confused.

ACTION STEP #2: Stay the course. Change is gradual. Remember the* Drops in the Bucket *to avoid frustration.

"Now," Brio said, "what do you think happens when, after six weeks of putting one drop of blue dye in a bucket of clear water every day, you still—after all that time—don't see any results?"

"Permission to speak frankly?"

"Granted," the owl nodded.

"Well, eventually, I would get very frustrated, and I would say this whole bucket idea is a load of zebra dung," responded Adir.

"That's right!" Brio exclaimed, willfully overlooking his student's uncouth nature. "The thing is, Adir, we live in a world of instant gratification, but we need to fight that pressure and remember that the worthiest goals take time and energy. If you get an *elephant buzz* by imagining your goal, then it's probably worth the time and effort it takes to realize that dream. When frustration sets in," Brio continued, "we start to second-guess ourselves. We think that maybe a different kind of dye might work, or we simply quit and move on to other projects."

57

We live in a **world** of **instant gratification**, but we need to **fight that pressure** and **remember** that the **worthiest goals** take **time** and **energy**.

At that point, Brio paused to give Adir time to consider these ideas. Adir thought about the last few weeks and all the times he had given up on Elgo. He had to admit that he had quit prematurely. He looked down at his notes: **Stay the course. Change is gradual.** He added a line that read, **_Learn to delay gratification._** Yet something still didn't sit right with the little guy.

"But wait a minute, Brio. Why didn't I see even the *tiniest* change in Elgo? He seemed determined to ignore my efforts. In fact, I got the distinct impression that he was unenthusiastic, unmotivated and even unwilling to cooperate."

"What was your strategy for keeping your elephant on track?" asked Brio. "What was your strategy for refocusing your efforts and turning things around when they got difficult?"

"Strategy? My strategy was to spend a minute or two imagining my future in the Oasis whenever the word *Oasis* came to mind," replied Adir.

"That approach will take you only so far . . ."

• • •

"Adir, what happened a few days ago when Elgo encountered a couple of lions?"

"Oh," said the tiny ant, his eyes widening, antennae stiffening. "Elgo was so fierce—he really scared them away."

"And then what?" Brio asked.

"And then we celebrated!"

"And then what? What did he see next?"

"Ohhh . . ." said Adir, beginning to realize where this lesson was going. "He heard a nest of mice and practically jumped out of his thick skin."

"Was he in danger?"

"From mice? Heck, no!" Adir said emphatically.

"But what was Elgo's truth?" Brio prodded.

"Elgo's truth was that those mice were totally and utterly terrifying."

"You see, Adir, Elgo's truth was not the same as your truth. Although you knew the mice posed absolutely no threat to a big creature like Elgo, his truth was very different."

"His truth nearly caused me to break my neck!"

"Adir, believe it or not, *you* are the one hindering progress toward the Oasis."

Adir did not like the direction of this conversation.

"Adir, what do you truly believe about the ease of getting to the Oasis?"

"It's not easy at all. It is so hard!"

"So you say to yourself: *My efforts will be a struggle.*"

"Yes. Yes, you're right," said Adir, dreading what was coming next.

"So the message you give yourself is really upside-down," said Brio. "Your truth about your journey to the Oasis is that it'll be a struggle. What if the truth is that it will be easy?"

"Well . . . it *could* be hard . . ." said Adir.

"Or not," said Brio. "The point is that everything you think—*your truth* about something—is transmitted to Elgo. If deep down you believe that getting to the Oasis is going to be an impossible struggle, then your teammate certainly won't be able to envision himself equipped to get there. "

"I suppose you're right," conceded Adir.

"No *elephant buzz* is going to take place when deep down you believe it will be a struggle to get to the Oasis. Every muscle in the elephant's body, beginning with the ten thousand muscles in his trunk, is going to behave as if getting to the Oasis were impossible. And who's responsible for that?"

"Me?" Adir said sheepishly.

The owl nodded his head and fixed his jewel-like eyes upon Adir, "Think of a friend who has a life you envy. How would you describe this creature?"

"Well, I have a monkey friend, Grant, who's carefree and enjoys life. Even when things are somewhat bleak, he seems to emerge with more abundance than before," said Adir wistfully.

"Tell me more about Grant and his struggles in life," said Brio.

"Well, Grant had a banana company that went bust; he lost everything. Yet three years later, his revived business flourished. He paid his debts and amassed even more bananas than he had before."

"This is very interesting," said Brio. "Why is it that monkeys like Grant can bounce back from negative situations, while other monkeys stay broke and never seem to bounce back?" asked the wise owl.

"The first group of monkeys has wealthy relatives?" joked Adir.

"But what if they don't?" responded Brio, once again failing to be amused.

Adir's forehead tensed as he tried to think of the answer. "Because Grant can envision himself with a lot of bananas, even when that's not really the current situation? And since *his reality* is that he can get a lot of bananas, everything he does turns into *more* bananas?"

"That's right! Grant has *vision*," said Brio. "But a lack of vision—some folks call it a *scarcity mentality*—isn't the only negative belief creatures carry around. From the tiniest caterpillar to the furriest gorilla, animals carry negative **beliefs**, **attitudes** and **truths** like heavy weights on their shoulders. This would drag anyone down after a while. Some creatures hold on to negative feelings about relationships, self-image, natural resources, traditions, authority figures, their neighbors, change, life . . . you name it!"

"Ouch," said Adir. "Sounds like a lot of creatures have negative perceptions that need some changing."

"Adir, there are some things you can't change, but more about life *can* be changed—from the inside out—than most folks realize. Focus positively on something long enough, keep moving, and you'll eventually get it."

"This is all very important, Brio. I think I need to write it down," Adir said with his twig in hand.

"But there's more," Brio said.

"Is there?"

"Certainly! Now, given everything we just discussed, it stands to reason, my brave little friend, that you'll be better off if you commit to an action step for maintaining positive, beneficial dominant thoughts. These thoughts will be your truth. And, if you can create a new truth—a truth that is in line with your vision—you'll be way ahead of the game."

61

"Is that it?" asked Adir apprehensively.

"Well, there's one thing you need to watch out for," responded Brio. "Your elephant is very literal, and you must choose your beliefs, attitudes and truths carefully."

"Can you give me an example?"

"Sure. Instead of *wanting* a place in the Oasis, I'd recommend that you focus on *having* a place in the Oasis. If you keep your focus on the want, you'll probably get nothing but a continued experience of wanting. Focus on having something, and you'll eventually have it."

"Hmmm," Adir said as he chewed pensively on his twig. "Very, very interesting."

"Let's use the example of an ant who wants to get a better job. This may sound like a small distinction, but if an ant continues to simply want a better job, his elephant will perceive the goal as wanting one, not having one. I know that the ant may end up with a job, but his chances are better if he changes his attitude and beliefs from *wanting* it to *envisioning himself already having attained* it."

Adir's little hand could barely keep up. ***Make a commitment to positive dominant thoughts. Shift beliefs, attitudes and truths so they are aligned with your vision. Envision having the goal rather than merely wanting the goal. Elgo's beliefs, attitudes and truths can be deeply held. You can change Elgo's mind with a dedicated, focused effort.***

"Your elephant, Adir, thinks in such a way that he will gravitate to whatever vision you consistently suggest to him. Your elephant is very literal and will only respond the way he was taught to. You need to commit to an ongoing process of specific, positive dialogue to enable the *elephant buzz* to work."

Brio smiled at the ant and yawned. "Adir, it's time for me to explore the area for a tree and enjoy a little siesta. But just for a few minutes, I'd like you to reflect on the times in your life when reality fell short of what you'd hoped and dreamed. Think about where your focus was prior to the events that left you disappointed."

Adir's Notes to Self

Commit to cultivating positive dominant thoughts.

- Shift beliefs, attitudes and truths so they are aligned with your vision.

- Envision *having* the goal, rather than merely *wanting* the goal.

- Elgo's beliefs, attitudes and truths can be deeply held. You can change Elgo's mind with a dedicated, focused effort.

  ACTION STEP #2: Stay the course. Change is gradual. Remember the Drops in the Bucket to avoid frustration. ***Learn to delay gratification.***

SUMMARY

1 | Clarify your vision.
ACTION: Find the emotion that ignites the vision. Inspire your team through emotion.

2 | Commit to cultivating positive dominant thoughts.
ACTION: Stay the course. Change is gradual.

8

Experiencing and Expressing Gratitude

Adir straightened up resolutely. He had made an important decision to stop focusing on what he could *not* do and start looking for ways to learn about himself and his abilities. He decided that his next move would be to innovate. He needed to create a tool to keep his focus on what he could do to get Elgo and himself to the Oasis.

What would the wise owl recommend? Adir thought to himself. He thought about how Brio would approach a problem. What steps would the owl take? *Well,* Adir thought, *the first thing he would do is put the problem into perspective. Before Brio would try to find a potential solution, he would devise a strategy.*

"That's it!" Adir cried, jumping up. "We need another action step, Elgo. We need a plan that will help us keep our goal in focus at all times!"

Adir thought about Brio's lessons. The more frequently he could stimulate an *elephant buzz*, the more likely he would be able to keep his truths in line with his dreams. The more his truths were in sync with his dreams, the more likely his elephant would stay on track.

"Strategy," said Adir out loud, hoping Elgo would get the message. "Strategy is the key for our team, Elgo. We need something to help us change what we believe is possible. When your truth and my truth are the same, we'll be able to get to the Oasis, but to create a new truth for you, we need something that will trigger a positive dominant thought in your mind. A reminder of the goal," Adir mused. "But what can we use to do that?"

Adir considered tying a small string around one of his legs. He imagined what this would be like and realized that the string would lose its novelty too quickly—it would be there all the time, and he would just get used to it. He needed something that would remind him and Elgo at various, unpredictable times throughout the day. He and Elgo needed a reminder that would surprise them and catch them off guard, pulling their minds back to center.

Just then a pollen spore drifted down from the sky and landed square on Adir's ant nose. He sneezed, brushed the golden powder from under his nose and suddenly froze.

"Under . . . my . . . nose," he whispered. "The answer is right under my nose!"

Adir gazed across Elgo's gray back. He noticed how other golden pollen spores were scattered here and there. He observed how the bright gold contrasted with the gray elephant skin.

"This could work, Elgo!" said Adir excitedly. "This could definitely work! Let's use these gold dots to trigger our dominant positive thoughts. Every time we see a gold dot of

66

pollen float through the air or land on something, it will remind us of our goal. These gold dots will make us think about *having* a place in the Oasis."

Elgo began to wave his trunk in approval. They were on to something.

• • •

For close to three weeks, Adir watched as the gold dots sailed down from the sky, reminding him about their goal of *having* a home in the Oasis. At first, these golden reminders were effective for both Adir and Elgo. Every time they saw one, images of the Oasis formed in their minds, and after a while, finding a golden pollen spore floating through the air became something of a game they played with each other.

Adir was almost obsessed with the gold dots. Each time he found a new one, he made sure to put it in a place where he was certain to see it. But while Adir was always championing the gold dot process, Elgo's mind began to wander; the elephant was still daydreaming about a variety of random things. It seemed to Adir that Elgo looked puzzled by the dots, as though he knew what they were but didn't know why he should care. Adir worried that Elgo would eventually forget all about what the gold dots were supposed to do and represent. He tried to remind Elgo, but the elephant was distracted. Maybe it was the gray skies and the still air of the savannah that caused doubt; Adir wasn't sure. He knew he wasn't going to give up, though.

This gold dot idea is a good one, he thought to himself. He pondered it for some time before saying to himself aloud, "What would Brio do now?"

Suddenly a booming voice inquired,

"Why don't you ask him?"

67

Adir was so startled he jumped straight up and spun around in mid-air.

"Aaah! You nearly gave me a heart attack, Brio!" Adir paused to catch his breath. "But, boy, am I glad you're back! I have so much to tell you!"*

Adir brought Brio up to date on everything that he had been working on in the owl's absence. He was particularly excited to tell Brio about his gold dot idea and get his feedback on why it seemed to stop working.

Brio listened intently and considered everything the ant said. "What exactly do you say to yourself when you see these gold dots?" he asked his pupil.

"Oh, well, usually I say something like: 'I can't wait to *have* a place in the Oasis,'" replied Adir.

"Excellent strategy, Adir. May I offer a suggestion? Three words, to be specific."

"Great! I'm all antennae." Adir grabbed his leaf and twig and readied himself for the next pearl of wisdom.

"Now. Gratitude. Experience," the owl said solemnly.

As usual, Adir wrote the concept before understanding what it meant. "Huh?"

"I'll explain," Brio said. "Make it *now*, add *gratitude* and briefly *experience* it," said Brio. "Let's start with what *making it now* means. The simple fact is that your gold dots will have more of an impact on Elgo if he registers them as real. Speaking in the present tense about something gives it definitive meaning to your subconscious. By speaking in the present tense, not only will you believe what you're saying, but you will convince your teammate to believe what you're saying, too. Confidently let him know that what you envision *is* a reality, albeit one that hasn't happened yet. So make it *now*, not something in the future. Give it a try."

---

* Like, for starters, don't sneak up on me anymore.

"I will live in the Oasis," said Adir seriously.

"That's a good start, but not quite right. Are you sure you want to use the word 'will' in your statement?" questioned Brio.

"Oh, I get it—'will' is not present tense. Okay, let me try again." Adir paused briefly before confidently announcing, "I *live* in the Oasis!"

"Good," said Brio. "Now, remind me of what living in the Oasis would be like. In other words, rekindle the *elephant buzz*."

The ant closed his eyes and let his vision play itself out in his mind's eye. "I'm on an anthill overlooking the Oasis, with a creek nearby. I have a family with me, and there are little ants running all around. They're happy and healthy. In the mornings, I go to work with my fellow ants, and we work hard, but we love what we do! I'm a great leader, and life is a grand adventure!" Adir opened his eyes, somewhat surprised by his own beautiful vision, and felt an enormous shudder from the elephant.

"Ah, yes," said Brio with a pleased expression, "an *elephant buzz* . . . but I bet we can give it a little more," said Brio. "Are you game?"

"Absolutely," Adir cried pumping his fist. "Bring it on!"

"Let's talk about your teammate, Elgo. Remember that your elephant has feelings and reasons for behaving the way he does. Most importantly, he's very receptive to all the information he's given. If you experience and express gratitude; you'll be able to keep your elephant on track. Not only will you be repeating a new truth to your teammate; you'll also be reinforcing it by creating a state of gratitude. Gratitude, Adir, is the magic ingredient in the recipe for a fulfilling life."

Gratitude is the magic ingredient in the recipe for a fulfilling life.

"Okay," said Adir, "how's this for a gold dot vision statement *with* gratitude: *I am grateful for our life in the Oasis.*"

"Perfect! Now imagine all the details in your vision. Experience them with all the senses of sight, sound, taste, touch and smell. Integrate the feeling of satisfaction you have because you've reached your goal," said Brio.

Adir did as Brio suggested. He closed his eyes and imagined his wonderful life in the Oasis as if he were living it right then and there. He could feel the sunshine and breeze, taste the delicious, clear water, see his friends and family, hear their happy chatter and smell the promise of great things. His heart swelled and his spirit sang. He was the luckiest ant in the world. The gentle buzzing beneath his feet increased with the richness of his vision. He opened his eyes contentedly and smiled at the owl.

"Very good, Adir," Brio said quietly. "You're making great progress." The owl readied himself to leave. "I'll return soon."

"Are you leaving? *Again?* So soon?" asked Adir.

"Yes, Adir, I'm going," Brio said

"But I still don't understand this lesson. What if I can't experience the vision without you here to guide me?" Adir worried.

Brio was already rising above him, flapping his wings. "Don't fear," responded Brio as he circled above. "You simply need to slow down and imprint all the wonderful details in your vision. As soon as you attach a specific, emotionally-charged thought to a gold dot, you will be sending clear, strong signals to your teammate."

Adir watched as the owl flew low and directly north over a less-traveled path. The heat off the ground began to distort the image of the flying bird, and the owl seemed to elongate and compress as he blurred into the distance. Eventually, the waves of heat consumed any view of the owl.

As soon as you attach a specific, emotionally-charged thought to a gold dot, you will be sending clear, strong signals to your teammate.

• • •

71

Brio was right, Adir did need to slow down. He needed to imprint all the wonderful details of his vision into his memory.

The gold dot concept was a good strategy, but it had to be refined to ensure that all of Adir's choices and actions remained connected to his goal. We could all learn something from the wise owl in this regard. When we set out to achieve a goal, we need to consistently focus on performance. For Adir, every time he saw that gold dot, he had to taste and feel the joys of being in the Oasis of his mind. More importantly, though, he needed to be grateful for his vision, his teammate and his own hard work.

Yes, Brio was right. Adir needed to understand the hazards of letting his goal float around like a feather in the wind. After all, how many such feathers end up in the Oasis?

He sat down with his twig and leaf and began taking notes about the things he had learned.

Adir's Notes to Self

LESSON #3

Consistently focus on performance.

- Experience the goal as though it were happening right now.

- Show your gratitude consistently.

  ACTION STEP #3: Use gold dot reminders. Gold dots are triggers for goals that have emotions tied to them. The personal gold dot must align with the gold dot of the team.

SUMMARY

1 | Clarify your vision.
ACTION: Find the emotion that ignites the vision. Inspire your team through emotion.

2 | Commit to cultivating positive dominant thoughts.
ACTION: Stay the course. Change is gradual.

3 | Consistently focus on performance.
ACTION: Use gold dot reminders.

Pattern Busters

It didn't take long for Elgo to return to lumbering along the usual path after Brio's departure. Adir gazed into the sky and wondered if he could catch a glimpse of the owl, but no such luck. Brio was gone, and their journey continued.

Adir looked forward, wondering exactly where the Oasis was. He turned to his left, where the sun rose every day. He thought it was funny that the sun always rose on the left side of the elephant path. Then a peculiar thought popped into his head.

What if the elephant were to walk along a different path? What would happen if the sun rose on the right side of the elephant? What if they followed the direction of the owl? How did that saying go? *The definition of insanity is doing the same thing over and over, expecting different results.*

"STOP!" yelled Adir urgently. "STOP, STOP, STOP!" Adir jumped up and down on the back of the elephant's head in a panic. He ran around in circles and nearly pulled out his antennae. He had seen a chance to change direction and knew they just had to take it. They had to be willing to try something new. They had to be willing to go another way.

After some hesitation, Elgo stopped.

"Please, Elgo, turn around," begged Adir.

The elephant started to turn and then, once again, stopped.

"Come on, Elgo. Turn around. You can do it!" urged Adir.

The elephant did just that. He rotated his enormous body in a complete 360-degree circle and ended up right where he began.*

"Whoa . . . stop, stop, stop," said Adir. "Turn around! Face the other way, Elgo. Face the other way, and *hold it right there!*"

The elephant did as he was told. As this was happening, Adir spotted a gold dot and had an idea. The moment the elephant was pointed north on the trail, the ant began to visualize all the details of the Oasis. He joined his elephant in imagining the lush, green environment. He smelled the fragrance of nature and heard the sounds of the creek and the other animals. He pictured the elephant bathing in the refreshing waters of the Oasis.

Suddenly there was an *elephant buzz*, and with this buzz Adir instructed the elephant to walk north. To his complete surprise, the elephant started walking north! Adir even sensed that the elephant was walking taller. He looked back and saw the elephant's tail swishing from side to side.

"Well!" Adir exclaimed. "That's either a sure sign of flies or one happy elephant!" In his current state of optimism, Adir decided it was the latter.

As they made their way along the path, Elgo occasionally slowed down as if he were hesitating or even attempting

---

* Like NASCAR, but slower.

to turn the other way again, but Adir remained patient and helped the elephant stay the course. Soon, it seemed as though Elgo knew the drill and could carry on without any assistance. Adir began to relax. *I could get used to this*, he thought to himself, stretching out. Adir felt as if he were just along for the ride.

That is, until the inevitable happened. Without any warning, Adir and Elgo came face to face with two elephants.

Adir instantly had a sinking feeling. He recognized the first elephant, Nega, a dour-looking creature with deep creases stemming from his frowning mouth. The second was none other than that miserable old elephant, Holic.

"Join us," they whined in unison. "You're going in the wrong direction. Think about it. We've just come from that direction, and there's nothing there. No Oasis, nothing. Do you think you'll find anything different? Come with us. Our names are Nega and Holic, and we love company."

Elgo instantly began to rub up against Nega and Holic. There was something familiar about them, and Elgo found it easy to simply reverse direction and go along with them.

Adir was startled at first, but his shock quickly turned into frustration, which quickly turned into anger.

"Wait a minute, Elgo," squeaked Adir. "They're not helping us take the path less-traveled! Think about it, Elgo! Why do they *love* company? Why, Elgo? Why?" Elgo continued to march on, and Adir continued to rant. "They *love company*, Elgo, because they're *miserable*; that's why!"

Adir's words succeeded only in slowing Elgo down. Before long, the ant and the elephant were back to the turn-around point. By this time it was dusk, and the group stopped for the night. Elgo prepared for sleep; it had been an exhausting day for the elephant.

75

Adir the ant, however, was wired with anxiety. Sleep did not come easily. No position felt comfortable. He thought how it was typical of elephants like Nega and Holic to show up and drag others down. *What is it with some creatures? Why do they have to hold others back?* Negative thoughts raced through his little ant brain. He tossed and turned and wondered why it was so difficult to get Elgo to move in a new direction. After all, he reasoned, that new direction might lead them to the Oasis! He imagined himself growing old on the back of a tired, old elephant. No colony, no friends, no family. His self-doubt doubled, and before long tripled, until eventually, a light sleep eclipsed the ant's thoughts.

• • •

Adir was climbing an endless staircase that rose high into the clouds of an ashen gray sky. But no matter how far he climbed, he didn't make any progress. At times, he would pause along the staircase to look back, but regardless of how hard he worked, he was no farther than halfway up the staircase at any point. Nothing seemed to make sense. Finally, he decided to turn around and go down. This time, the valley floor never got any closer. It was the worst feeling of futility the ant had ever experienced. He began to cry out, "NO! NO! NO!"

"You might be better off using the phrase, 'No, thank you,'" said a familiar voice.

Adir immediately opened his eyes and realized he was in bed. The sun was rising behind the outline of Brio's strong physique, and with the glow of light beyond him, there seemed to be a golden aura around the proud bird's frame.

"Good morning, Adir," boomed Brio.

"What did you say to me?" asked Adir groggily.

"Good morn . . ."

"No," interrupted Adir. "Sorry, not that. When I was sleeping, what did you say?"

"Oh, I said that you'd be better off using the phrase 'No, thank you.'"

Adir looked at the outline of the owl and then lay back, closing his eyes again.

"Brio, I don't feel that hot right now. I got maybe ten minutes of sleep last night, and yesterday my emotions were up and down like a yo-yo. This whole business of getting my elephant to pay attention is like trying to get a hyena to stop cackling!"

"*Uh, uh, uhhhhh,*" admonished the owl. "It's not impossible." The owl paused to study his student. "Adir, when your mind is plagued with negative thoughts, what do you do?" Brio asked.

Adir sat upright. "That's what I was going to ask you. I kept having this half-awake dream that I was climbing an endless staircase, but when I wanted to start climbing down again, it never seemed to end, and I couldn't get to the bottom! I was stuck! I knew I was dreaming, but I was powerless to stop or change it." Adir flopped down again. "I am so *stressed out!*"

"Adir," Brio said calmly, "you need to take a deep breath and relax. Deep breathing is a good thing to do when you feel your stress level rise."

77

Deep breathing is a good thing to do when you feel your stress level rise.

Adir did as Brio suggested. He steadied himself with his breath and waited for the owl to continue.

"What did you do when you couldn't change direction on the staircase? Did you give up?"

"No, I didn't give up, but the dream kept going until I woke up. Well, actually, until you woke me up . . . but now that I think about it, there are times when negative thoughts seem similar to an endless staircase. Sometimes I feel like I never seem to get anywhere."

"Well," Brio said, "what do you do then?"

"I try to think of something else."

"Does it work?"

"Sometimes it works for me—but my teammate down there," Adir said, pointing at the elephant's back, "is a bit more stubborn, if you catch my drift."

"I see. Well, let me share my formula for fixing frustration with you. The idea is to find a way to turn around negative thoughts that hinder your—or Elgo's—attention."

"Great idea, Mr. Brio, but it's not that easy," interjected the ant. "For a time, I would think of my *elephant buzz*, but then all of a sudden I'd be thinking about how I was still unable to find the Oasis. Whenever I'd think that, I'd think about how past generations must have struggled to find the Oasis. I'd think about how tough life is and how hard it'll continue to be. Before long, I'd be down, deflated, wondering how I got here."

"I understand, Adir," said Brio, who had counseled many other animals and knew how challenging it was to establish new patterns of thought. "This formula can help you, and I think you'll like it." The owl was about to explain the theory, but cleared his throat and paused. "Uh, Adir? You might want to get your twig and leaf ready for this one."

"Right!" said Adir, nodding affirmatively. "Will do!"

"So," the owl began when Adir was ready, "in your dream, you were climbing an endless staircase where nothing made sense. You could not reach the top or the bottom. One thing I've learned in many years of discussing dreams with other creatures is that stairs often represent a struggle to reach something better—a goal, such as the Oasis—and the steps can represent repetition, or a pattern." The owl eyed his student. "Do you follow?"

"Not really," said Adir, furrowing his brow.

"Allow me to continue. In your dream you kept going up and down the stairs, but felt you weren't progressing. You were stuck in a pattern that was getting you nowhere."

"That's true!"

"The way it works, Adir, is that one negative thought leads to another and another and another. This chain of negativity is a pattern." Brio adjusted his booming voice so that is was whiny, squeaky and anxious—kind of like Adir's, actually. "You might think: 'The oasis is too tough to reach . . .' This thought leads to: 'This has been a fact of life for generations. Woe is me. There's nothing I can do about it.' Then you might link this thought to: 'We ants are destined to struggle . . .,' which is a pattern of thought linked to: 'I'm not good enough . . .,' and so on."

The chain of negativity is a pattern.

Brio let what he said, and the voice he used to say it, resonate for Adir before continuing. "Negative thoughts erode your confidence, Adir, and when it comes to realizing your goals, this is something you simply can't afford. In order to restore confidence in your ability, you need to replace your negative thoughts with positive ones."

"Wow, Brio, I feel like this lesson was specifically designed for me!"

"Adir, you aren't alone. Lots of creatures could learn from this lesson. If you learn to apply a formula to interrupt this kind of negative pattern, you'll be able to catch yourself before your thoughts spiral out of control. This will take some practice, though. At first, you will be able to interrupt the pattern only after you have been in it for a time. Eventually, you'll learn to catch yourself before those negative thoughts get the best of you."

The owl paused to collect his thoughts. "Now, where was I? Oh, yes. Adir, there's a simple law of physics that says: *No two things can occupy the same space at the same time.* Equally true, no two *thoughts* can occupy your elephant's mind at the exact same time."*

80

Adir was scribbling faster than he had ever scribbled before—*no two things, same place, same time . . .*

"When you find yourself in this situation, the best thing to do is to say the following: 'Thank you, but that is not part of my vision. My vision is that I live in the Oasis.' Then, again, visualize the glorious details of the Oasis with all five of your senses."

Adir spoke the words aloud as he wrote them down. *"Thank you, but that is not part of my vision. My vision is that I **live** in the Oasis."*

"Very good. Your task in the coming days is to give this a try whenever you think negative thoughts. Stop yourself, and say to Elgo, *"Thank you, but that is not part of my vision. My vision is a home in the Oasis."* Then see how things change. Once you consistently use this formula, you

* Also, *always double down on a split pair in Vegas* and the lesser-known, *no two Baldwin brothers should act in the same movie.*

will be able to redirect your elephant to think positively rather than negatively. The more you interrupt a pattern, the less it will have a footing in his mind. Over time, the pattern will disappear. You'll effectively change the overall complexion of your thoughts. As you learn to recognize those pesky negative patterns, you'll interrupt them earlier and earlier. Before long they'll be gone, and you and Elgo will think only positively."

As you **learn** to **recognize** **negative** patterns, you will **interrupt** them **earlier** and **earlier**.

81

Adir took Brio's explanation of thought patterns to heart. He knew that before he could change Elgo's bad habits, he needed to understand and recognize his own behavior. He needed to curb his own negative thoughts as soon as they began. If he did this, he would be able to get positive results from Elgo. It was beginning to dawn on Adir that his behavior as a leader affected his elephant in ways he had never imagined. By just thinking positively, he would be able to lead his elephant by example.

• • •

One day, not long after this lesson with Brio, Adir was having trouble finding where he had stored some seeds for later munching.

"I don't believe it! I know I put them right here," he muttered grumpily to himself. "I hope that big, old lug Elgo didn't sniff them out and eat them! How am I ever going to find the Oasis if I can't even find where I stored my food?"

After an hour or so of searching, he began to sing an even more pessimistic tune: "I'll never get to the Oasis. This is all so pointless! I'm just a dumb ant! I can't lead Elgo. Who am I kidding? I might as well give up right now . . ."

But then he stopped, right there in the midday sun.

"Wait a minute!" Adir exclaimed to the open sky. "I can't think like this! This negative talk isn't going to get me to the Oasis!"

Adir closed his eyes, paused and said in a clear and deliberate voice, "Thank you, but that is not part of my vision. My vision—our vision—is a beautiful, comfortable, wonderful home in the Oasis."

Adir imagined the vibrating energy of the Oasis. In his mind, he joked with the friendly creatures. He thought about walking amidst the lush, green vegetation, pausing to contemplate the rippling lake. He watched the sunshine play upon the forest floor in a dazzling ballet of shadow and light. As Adir's vision unfurled, he heard a symphony of sound. In his mind's fertile ground, he could feel it, taste it, touch it, smell it and see it.

He thought about the happy, joyous atmosphere of the Oasis, and as a result of all these positive thoughts, he felt a long, wonderful *elephant buzz*. With his mind clear and positive, Adir found where he had hidden the seeds in no time at all.

Adir repeated the formula Brio taught him every time he noticed a negative thought trying to take over. Before long, Adir realized that Elgo seemed to wander about less. Deep down in his tiny ant bones, Adir could sense they were getting closer.

Adir's Notes to Self

Strengthen confidence.

- Frustration will lead to negative thoughts. Negative thoughts add fuel to more negativity. This negativity can be a pattern that destroys confidence.

- No two thoughts can occupy the mind at the same time. Replace negativity with positive, confident thoughts.

  ACTION STEP #4: Institute pattern busters. Once you recognize yourself or your team playing out the pattern of negativity, interrupt this thought by saying, "Thank you, but that is not part of my vision. My vision is . . ." Experience the vision in detail.

SUMMARY

1 | Clarify your vision.
ACTION: Find the emotion that ignites the vision. Inspire your team through emotion.

2 | Commit to cultivating positive dominant thoughts.
ACTION: Stay the course. Change is gradual.

3 | Consistently focus on performance.
ACTION: Use gold dot reminders.

4 | Strengthen confidence.
ACTION: Institute pattern busters.

Expecting the Unexpected

A few days later, as the sun was setting over the western plains of the savannah, Brio flew back to meet with Adir. In flight, Brio looked around and noticed how the shadows mixed with the deep orange glow from a setting sun. The sunset was a gentle reminder that another day had passed. Brio enjoyed this time of day; it signified how life was full of opportunities either gained or lost. Sunsets symbolized one question to Brio: what choices would tomorrow offer? As he spied Adir and Elgo in the distance, the owl couldn't help but wonder what choices his two friends would make after learning the next lesson.

• • •

After settling on Elgo's back, Brio paused and looked the ant up and down. Adir, like most ants, was inclined to pursue instant gratification. His mentor knew in advance that this next strategy would not be as easy for Adir to implement. After a few contemplative moments, Brio began his lesson.

"What I am about to explain to you is, quite frankly, the very best technique you can use to get your elephant to change directions. It's an amazing strategy for building and strengthening your confidence and sense of control. This one technique, Adir, could change your life."

"Let me get my leaf and twig!" the ant cried.

"Hold on one minute. Before I tell you about this action step, there's a problem you should know about." Brio paused. "I'm afraid that the chance of your following through with this is slim unless you're one hundred percent committed to reaching your goal."

"Committed? Brio, I am committed," said Adir as he poked his tiny ant thumb into his chest.

"Committed, perhaps, but are you willing to redefine commitment and take it to a level of maturity and action beyond anything you've ever known?" *

"Well, if you put it that way . . ." the ant murmured with intimidation.

"You see, Adir, commitment is active. It's judged on a sliding scale. We can reach a level of commitment and discover there's still more we can do. The monkey we spoke about earlier, for instance, could start a business and then realize his commitment involved more than he had anticipated. Or, perhaps we discover mid-way through a project that more dye is needed to make that bucket of water blue. The truth is, Adir, you can always dig deeper and find a more profound level of commitment. Being committed to a task means, in effect, being committed to the process of commitment. I want you to promise me—no, strike that, *promise yourself*—that when you think you've done all you

* Cue dramatic music.

can possibly do, you'll dig even deeper into the coconut's core. When you've fulfilled the commitment you established for yourself, *commit even further*."

Being committed to a task means, in effect, being committed to the process of commitment.

"I promise!" Adir said, dizzy with inspiration. "I'll commit to the process of commitment!"

"You must do whatever it takes," said Brio, bending his head down to the rough, gray elephant hide and looking into Adir's eyes. "When it comes to reaching your goal, follow-through is of utmost importance."

"I will!"

"Good!" said Brio, satisfied that Adir understood how important follow-through was. "Adir, as we've discussed your goal of getting to the Oasis, most of our action steps have involved visualizing the life you dream of. Now I want to introduce you to a different technique."

"But, Brio, what if I work really hard at this new technique, yet can't get Elgo to buy in to it?"

"Adir, you underestimate your elephant and yourself as his leader. Look at all the tools you've learned to use so far. Get out your notes, and let's take a moment to review them."

87

Together, Brio and Adir went through the lessons:

Make fear your friend, not your master. You don't know what you don't know.

"First, you clarified your vision. You discovered that fear can either cripple or motivate. You learned how to manage fear and use it to your advantage. You opened up to the possibility that you don't know what you don't know. You did not know that you'd been living on the back of an elephant, but once you did, you accepted it and decided to meet the challenge. You then had to decide what your goal would be and prepare yourself to take the necessary steps to reach that goal."

Zero in on a goal that has a depth of meaning. The journey has to be worth taking.

"After identifying your goal—living in the Oasis—you defined the core reasons why it was so important to you. You kept asking yourself why you want to live in the Oasis because you learned that the journey had to mean something to you; otherwise, there would be no reason to put all the hard work into realizing it. Without a clarified vision and an emotional investment, you wouldn't have been able to make the commitment needed to achieve your goal."

ACTION STEP #1: Find the *elephant buzz*. Find the emotion that ignites the vision. Inspire your team through emotion. _Never underestimate the power of emotion._

"Adir, in this first lesson you learned that your emotions are powerful motivators for both you and your teammate, Elgo. Harness the power of your emotions, and the world is yours. Also, you learned that you need to consider what motivates your teammate as much as you consider what motivates you. You need to use those dreams and desires to inspire him."

• • •

Commit to cultivating positive dominant thoughts. Shift beliefs, attitudes and truths so they are aligned with your vision. Envision having the goal rather than merely wanting the goal.

"Next you realized how important your thoughts and actions are to your teammate. You made a commitment to nurturing positive dominant thoughts. You realized, too, that you need to lead and direct Elgo through beliefs, attitudes and truths that are in sync with your goal. You discovered that *wanting* something and *having* something are two different things. If you're truly going to lead Elgo to the Oasis, you need to envision having something. This way, you'll lead Elgo by example and train him to think positively. With time, his beliefs, attitudes and truths will reflect those positive thoughts, as well."

89

ACTION STEP #2: Stay the course. Change is gradual. Remember the *Drops in the Bucket* to avoid frustration. <u>Learn to delay gratification.</u>

"In this second lesson, you realized that in a world where we're always tempted by instant gratification, real, profound change tends to come slowly. When you're trying to inspire Elgo to change, you're correcting a lifetime of behavior. Be patient; stay the course; don't become frustrated. If you're committed to the vision, you'll achieve it in time."

• • •

Experience your future with gratitude as though it were happening right now. Show your gratitude consistently.

"Adir, you invented and mastered the concept of gold dots. In doing so, you came to see that complaining would not get you very far. Instead, you opted for experiencing and expressing gratitude; you now know that gratitude is the magic ingredient in the recipe for a fulfilling life. Now, each time you see a gold dot, you're filled with the thought of your goal, you experience the goal as though you have just attained it, and you thank yourself for having reached the goal. You also learned that by helping Elgo, you help yourself, so you always have to thank Elgo, too, for the role he played in reaching the goal."

ACTION STEP #3: Use gold dot reminders. Gold dots are triggers for goals that have emotions tied to them. The personal gold dot must align with the gold dot of the team.

"Remember, Adir, gold dots offer you two reminders: the first is that you'll gravitate toward your current dominant thought, and the second is that you'll come to believe this thought to be true. These gold dots will keep your dominant thoughts aligned and on target. Repeat these thoughts often enough, and you'll create a truth. You'll paint a reality that will eventually happen."

• • •

Strengthen confidence. Frustration will lead to negative thoughts. Negative thoughts fuel more negativity. This negativity can be a pattern that destroys confidence. No two thoughts can occupy the mind at

the same time. Replace negativity with positive, confi-
dent thoughts.

"In our most recent lesson, you realized how negative patterns erode your confidence, and that without confidence, you won't be able to stay the course and realize your objective. When you find yourself indulging negative thought patterns, recall that old rule of physics: *No two things can occupy the same place at the same time.* You need to clear away the negative ideas in order to nurture the positive ones. You learned a powerful technique to do just that."

ACTION STEP #4: Institute pattern busters. Once you recognize yourself or your team playing out the pattern of negativity, interrupt the pattern by saying, "Thank you, but that is not part of my vision. My vision is . . ." Experience the vision in detail.

"Adir, with this last action step, you discovered a way to redirect your thinking with a positive twist, stopping negative thoughts in their tracks. With this technique, you'll no longer suffer from negativity, but you'll strengthen your confidence and focus on your dreams. The future you seek is a reality that just hasn't happened yet!"

● ● ●

Adir studied his list. He was astonished by how much he had learned from the wise owl. "We have covered a lot of ground, Brio."

"Yes, we certainly have!" The owl spread his impressive wings, flapped them up and down several times and shook his beautiful, feathery head. "And guess what, Adir?"

"What?" the tiny ant asked.

91

"Your lessons," whispered Brio, "are almost done!"

• • •

"Let's continue with a new action step. I call this one the *Flash Card Technique*. This is where you use flash cards to prepare for stressful situations that inevitably pop up as you follow the path to a goal. This kind of preparation helps you build **confidence** and **control**, and as you probably know, *confidence comes from experience*. A stack of flash cards will simulate multiple experiences, preparing you to handle any kind of situation. Knowing that you can handle any situation will ultimately deliver great results. The best part is that you'll shortcut the struggle of learning the hard way— the way of trial and error. In this case, your task is to write at least ten worst-case scenarios, one on each flash card."

Adir looked up from his notes. This was a technique he could really get into. "Like what?" he asked attentively.

"Situations or circumstances which, if they happened in real life, would cause you a great deal of anxiety. For example, think about what happened with Nega and Holic. What was your confidence level when faced with this difficult situation?" asked Brio.

"My confidence? I had no confidence!" said Adir. "But how could I have predicted such a scenario?"

"Precisely, my little ant! The idea here is to let the flash cards predict a variety of scenarios that *could* happen so you can handle the unpredictable ones that *do* happen," said Brio. "If you use this technique to build a broad foundation of confidence, you'll be ready to take action without hesitation when unpredictable situations occur. The point is to visualize how *well* you would handle a bad situation."

Brio began to pace back and forth as he continued to

speak. "For instance, one flash card could read: 'As you approach the Oasis, you are extremely excited. Then you peek around the corner and discover that the Oasis has dried up and that no one is there. You're overwhelmed with frustration and a profound desire to give up—'" The owl swiveled his head around, looked directly at the ant and spoke rapidly: "Adir, what would you do?"

"I don't know exactly!" Adir exclaimed, taken aback. "What would be the right thing to do in this situation?"

"Ah . . . yes." The owl beamed, enjoying the startled expression on the ant's face. "That's the beauty of this technique. The perfect solution is not the point. The point is to simply give yourself an imagined experience—any experience—of solving the problem. Take your best guess and then experience it. More experience will result in more confidence and control. Remember our analogy of the bucket of blue water? Each time you flip through a flash card, you're adding another drop of blue dye to your bucket. By itself it will not make a big difference, but cumulatively—well! You can imagine the impact. Visualizing hundreds of scenarios in which you handle tough situations will build a rock-solid platform to help you reach your goal."

"But," said Adir with hesitation, "I don't really think that imagining an experience is the same as the real thing." *

"Actually, Adir, the imagined experience is very powerful. Think back to a time when someone said something nasty and mean to you. Perhaps you didn't know what to say at the time, but within seconds of walking away, you probably replayed the experience in your mind and thought of the perfect retort. Chances are you replayed that nasty exchange in your mind over and over, and each time you thought of an even better response."

93

---

* Unless the real thing that you're talking about is imagining something. But that's just weird.

"Actually," Adir mused, "that sounds pretty accurate."

"Doesn't it?" Brio smiled. "Let's take an example. What did that disagreeable crow say to you when you asked him if he could take you to the Oasis?"

"Oh, yeah!" Adir mimicked the crow's nasal voice: *"And precisely why, little ant, would I do that?* Oh, Brio, I've replayed that situation a bunch of times! If I see him again, I'm going to march right up to him and say, 'Hey! Daffy Duck called. He wants his outfit back.'"

"How many times did you actually have a conversation with the crow, Adir?"

"Once."

"But how many times did you *experience* it?"

"Dozens . . . if not hundreds," said Adir.

"So you see, the flash card technique is not so different from that run-in you had with the crow. But in this case, it is a positive, constructive way to experience something unpleasant and to build your levels of confidence and control."

"Brio, sir, this is a fantastic idea," Adir said, grinning.

"Trust me, Adir. It really works. Now, what's your next step?"

"Me? My next step would be to write up a few flash cards," said Adir.

"When?" asked Brio.

"Today," the ant responded.

"How many flash cards will you come up with?"

"Uh," Adir tallied the number in his head, "ten?"

"Perfect," said Brio as he ruffled his feathers, preparing to fly away. "I must go now to see what's for dinner. I'll be back sometime tomorrow, and we can see how your flash card exercise went."

Adir's Notes to Self

Control the response to any situation.

- Unforeseen circumstances will arise. Expect
  the unexpected. Anticipate your response to
  challenges as well as your team's.

  ACTION STEP #5: Use flash cards. Design
  flash cards that detail stressful scenarios.
  Mentally experience handling these stressful
  situations with ease.

SUMMARY

1 | Clarify your vision.
ACTION: Find the elephant buzz. Find the emotion
that ignites the vision.

2 | Commit to cultivating positive dominant
thoughts.
ACTION: Stay the course. Change is gradual.

3 | Consistently focus on performance.
ACTION: Use gold dot reminders.

4 | Strengthen confidence.
ACTION: Institute pattern busters.

5 | Control the response to any situation.
ACTION: Use flash cards.

Later the next day, Brio returned as promised. The owl found Adir waiting with a smug expression on his face.

"Well, you look pleased with yourself, my little friend," Brio said. "Tell me, did the flash cards go well?"

"Ah, well, only if you call, oh, just about twenty-one gah-lorious, pattern-busting, stress-filled flash cards good!" said Adir as he raised a little ant eyebrow. "Let's see. Number one: A mouse jumps out from behind a log and scares Elgo. With skill and poise, what do I do? Number two: A fire appears on the horizon, and Elgo doesn't know which way to turn. How do I handle the situation with confidence? Number three: We come across Nega, Holic and their cousins, Miz, Ery, Badatt and Itude. Elgo desperately wants to join in with them. How do I turn the situation around?"

"Impressive," responded Brio. "You definitely have what it takes. Nothing makes me happier than to see you take the extraordinary steps to learn new strategies and tools. You see, the ordinary steps are what most ants take. And ordinary results are what they get. *Extraordinary steps*, however, produce *extraordinary results*."

Extraordinary steps produce extraordinary results.

"But why don't all ants take extraordinary steps so they get extraordinary results?" Adir asked. This was one thing that continued to nag him. Why hadn't he learned these techniques back at the colony? If someone had taught him some of these ideas, he might have been a better ant and a better leader for his team.

"Good question. The answer is only one word," Brio said. *"Fear!"*

"I thought so!" interrupted Adir, nodding his head.

"We could also call it an elephant fear. As you recognize the feeling of fear, ask yourself in a rational way, 'Would I rather reach my goals or stay afraid?' There are countless examples throughout history of how the courageous obtain rewards that the timid will never know. Fear can keep us safe and secure, but it can also keep us ignorant. Think of the best lessons that you have learned in your life. When you learned these important life-lessons, Adir, were you comfortable or uncomfortable?"

Adir took a moment to consider the question. He thought about how uncomfortable he was when he was promoted by the Queen. He was so afraid that he was going to do a bad job, that he did a bad job! He realized how many invaluable lessons he had learned since his separation from the colony. These were lessons that he wouldn't have learned if he had returned home, even though that was what he had wanted to do. And the past few months had been some of the most uncomfortable the little ant had ever known.

"I see where my fear has gotten the best of me in the past, and if there is any proof that discomfort and learning important lessons often go hand in hand, well, these past months prove it!"

"I'm not surprised," said Brio, "That's why you need to be willing to experience the discomfort you're sure to encounter as you journey on to the Oasis."

"That doesn't sound easy," said Adir in a flat voice, "or very pleasant."

"Easy is the comrade of the timid! Adir, it's time for you to put all that you've learned to the test. It's out there," said Brio as he pointed in a sweeping motion across the savannah. "That's where you truly will be able to practice what you've learned. Trust in yourself as I trust in you. I know that you'll take the extraordinary steps you need to in order to achieve great and wonderful things."

With that, Brio gave his wings three quick flaps. Maximizing the updraft off the large elephant's back, Brio appeared almost weightless as he lingered a few meters over the ant's head. He spoke his parting words:

> As you live your life, you'll realize the importance of living without regret over what might have been. Will you look back and wonder if you could've done more? Will you look back and question whether you gave it everything you had? If you can look back and have no regrets, you'll know that you did your best, and your best can take you to places beyond your wildest expectations.

99

Brio gave his wings an effortless shift. With each stroke of his powerful wings, he soared higher. He spoke three last words that echoed in Adir's ears for years to come: "Have no regrets!"

12

A New Beginning

Adir looked up at the sky. It had been a week since his last lesson with the wise owl. He was still desperately lonely, and he still ached to find his fellow ants and get back to his colony, but now there was something different. He sensed a reserve of strength inside his little body, and this filled him with a sense of pride and accomplishment. Great things were about to happen—he could just feel it!

He knew that he wouldn't ever see Brio again, but he would never forget him. Adir decided to honor everything the wise owl had taught him, and to do that, he refined his notes into a short list he could always refer to when he needed help to stay on track. As he sat with the twig and leaf, he realized that Brio's concepts resulted in a list of five all-important "C" words. *This sure will make them easy to remember*, he thought to himself.

ADIR'S FIVE C'S:

1. **CLARITY OF VISION: A goal with a depth of meaning has an emotional buzz.**

2. **COMMITMENT: Commit to a process of positive dominant thoughts.**

3. **CONSISTENCY: Apply consistent strategies. (The bucket will turn blue.)**

4. **CONFIDENCE: Strengthen confidence by breaking negative patterns.**

5. **CONTROL: Practice responses to the unforeseen events that may arise.**

LIST OF ACTION STEPS

* **ACTION STEP #1: Find the *elephant buzz*. Find the emotion that ignites the vision. Inspire your team through emotion. Never underestimate the power of emotion.**

* **ACTION STEP #2: Stay the course. Change is gradual. Remember the *Drops in the Bucket* to avoid frustration. Learn to delay gratification.**

* **ACTION STEP #3: Use gold dot reminders. Gold dots are triggers for goals that have emotions tied to them. The personal gold dot must align with the gold dot of the team.**

* **ACTION STEP #4: Institute pattern busters. Once you recognize yourself or your team playing out the pattern of negativity, interrupt the pattern by saying, "Thank you, but that is not part of my vision. My vision is . . ." Experience the vision in detail.**

* **ACTION STEP #5: Use flash cards. Design flash cards that detail stressful scenarios. Mentally experience handling these stressful situations with ease.**

Just knowing he had these ideas and action steps put a smile on the ant's tiny face.

• • •

Adir studied his lists every day, and slowly but surely the concepts and action steps became part of his daily life. He knew he would see results by shifting the beliefs, attitudes and truths surrounding his chance of reaching the Oasis. Every day he would imagine putting another drop of blue dye in the bucket of water. He would feel one small, imperceptible step closer to his goal: finding the Oasis.

Adir also decided to implement a gold dot reminder that would give him an *elephant buzz*. He decided that the gold dot statement would begin with gratitude. Each time he saw a gold dot he said "thank you" to Elgo for his continued effort; he also thanked himself for staying the course. Adir further decided to be grateful for everything that he presently had in life.

Finally, Adir decided to head off negative thoughts, stress and fear by using the action steps he learned. He reminded his elephant that negativity had to be replaced by their beautiful vision of the Oasis. He trained his elephant to handle stressful scenarios with flash cards designed to build confidence and dissolve fear. Also, he was willing to experience discomfort in order to reach his goal.

• • •

The first weeks after Brio's last visit were tough for Adir. Elgo was a formidable challenge, and change did not come easily. There were moments when Adir caught himself getting dragged down by negative patterns. Negative thoughts oozed back into his mind, and negativity seemed to be a familiar playground for his teammate.

At times, Adir would look around the path they were on and realize that Elgo was going the wrong way. Going the wrong way seemed natural to Elgo; the elephant would continue to march in the direction he recognized. Only when the determined ant stepped in would things change, and sometimes only temporarily.

Unbeknownst to Adir, the wise owl kept watch over the little ant and his elephant from high above. Brio knew the many challenges Adir faced as he continued to practice and incorporate these teachings into his daily life. It is horribly frustrating to keep working at something without immediate results, and the owl knew that there were days when Adir was overwhelmed by that frustration.

Still, as Brio watched from the limb of a tree, or as he trailed behind Elgo and Adir, undetected by either one, he saw their progress slowly take shape. As he had known all along, this ant was not going to give up. He was using the many skills Brio taught him, and more importantly, he was learning from them as he practiced. Small differences—differences that might go undetected by you or me—were not overlooked by the owl. Slowly and haltingly, the negative patterns were changing. Brio could see wonderful new habits emerging in the elephant.

Think how remarkable this is! Elgo had grown up knowing only struggle. Generations of pachyderms before him had been trapped in a fight just to survive. Of course, Elgo had not chosen this mentality intentionally—like many of us, his way of thinking was learned and inherited. Nevertheless, Elgo had accepted long ago that his existence was something that had to be endured, and he let that idea be his compass. Now, though, Adir was gently guiding and encouraging him to go in new directions, toward his bliss.

Without Adir, Elgo would have been helpless to change. And without Elgo's power, Adir never would have even thought the Oasis was a possibility. These two creatures were the most unlikely friends, but this tiny ant and this enormous elephant needed one another.

Brio was proud of his students. He looked down upon them one last time and knew they would achieve anything they set their minds to. Together, they would continue to make progress.

• • •

Weeks passed, but Adir never gave up. His gold dots reminded him of his goal to reach the Oasis. Slowly he began to recognize that each day he was moving closer to his life-long dream. The landscape gradually changed from dry and brown to patches of green. Landmarks like the withered shrubs became less frequent. In their place, the landscape included lush trees and patches of wildflowers.

The best part was the way it felt to Elgo. The big elephant seemed to walk more lightly and freely. There was a feeling of resonance between ant and elephant, and Adir began to realize that Elgo, given the chance, knew the right course of action. Given the opportunity, the inner instinct of the elephant was in harmony with what both creatures really wanted. With this alignment, it was as if the sun were shining more vibrantly and the birds were singing more melodiously. Even the breeze coming across the landscape seemed more refreshing. Without Adir and Elgo even recognizing it, everything seemed to change for the better. *Huh!* Adir thought, *I feel like the bucket is actually becoming blue!*

One night the sky seemed particularly clear, and the stars sparkled with a rare brilliance. With his front legs folded behind his head, Adir lay on his back and started to reminisce aloud.

"You know, Elgo, life is pretty strange! One minute I am working my six legs off to be a good leader—and not doing a great job of it—and the next, I find out I've been living on your back all along! Next thing I know, I meet Brio the Wise Owl! I still can't believe that; I mean, he is *really famous*! Then we're following Nega and Holic to who knows where, but tonight we can see so far into the distance that anything seems possible."

Adir took a deep breath of the crisp night air. He held in the breath and let the rich oxygen course through his little veins.* Perhaps the feeling of happiness was temporary, Adir mused, but the profound feeling of fulfillment reverberated from his heart to his extremities. Adir had never felt more alive.

He exhaled slowly and took another deep breath. The clean, still air permeated every cell in his body. As he slowly exhaled again, he gazed upward and whispered, "Thank you."

Despite the late hour, the ant could not sleep. The trees surrounding them were strong sentinels of the night protecting its inhabitants. There was a quiet calm as nature replenished herself with rest for a new day. Nevertheless, Adir and Elgo were awake, neither knowing nor caring why. It was a perfect night for a silent celebration of life itself.

Adir continued to let his thoughts drift. He remembered the times when his family was together, before he had to "grow up." He recalled those innocent days of his young anthood. Then he found himself reminiscing about his recent

107

---

* By this time you should know better than to ask questions. Ants can write and talk, they do the twist, and yes, they have veins. Really, really little veins.

struggles at the colony and the disappointment he had experienced in himself as a leader. It had seemed so overwhelming at the time, and yet now it seemed so remote. He recognized how he had grown, thanks to his friend and mentor, Brio. As if it were echoing in his imagination, he heard the familiar sound of Brio's voice whispering, "Have no regrets!" Given the opportunity to lead his fellow ants now, Adir knew he would be able to make a really positive impact.

Then, switching to his conscious thought, he heard something else. Adir raised his head and looked west into the shadows toward a fairly big hill. He listened carefully, but the sound disappeared. Still, his curiosity was piqued.

After a few moments Adir said, "Come on, Elgo. Let's check it out."

Despite the late hour, Elgo rose to the occasion and headed west off the main trail and toward the hill. As they walked along, Adir knew they were leaving the well-worn path in the shadows behind them. The stars were so bright they cast an ethereal light—just enough to guide them to the hill. Pretty soon the untracked territory made Elgo somewhat uncomfortable.

"C'mon, Elgo. Let's just see what's on the other side of the hill; then we can decide what we want to do next."

Elgo continued to march forward, gaining confidence with every step. The hill itself was not steep; it had a gentle, inviting slope. As Elgo marched on, Adir looked back and started to gain perspective. The higher they climbed, the more of the landscape he could see. Even though it was somewhat dark, a glow from the sky revealed a panoramic view from north to south. Adir and Elgo's walk up the hill revealed the impressive journey they had traveled. Adir could make out the exact elephant path that they had taken for years. He could also make out the turning point at which he and Elgo had left Nega and Holic up to their own devices—and vices.

As Adir tried to make out some more landmarks, he suddenly felt an amazing shudder from Elgo. It was an *elephant buzz.*

Immediately, Adir jumped up, ran to the top of Elgo's head and froze in his tracks. He could not believe his eyes.

There, spanning a few hundred acres, was a huge, lush forest of trees surrounding a body of calm water. The pond mirrored the stars above and reflected light in all directions. It was as if the sky and pond had conspired to bring the heavens to earth. A deep green permeated every corner of the expanse. The forest floor was a blanket of ferns spreading across the entire basin. To their left was a small, natural spring creek that flowed effortlessly down the other side of the hill.

109

Adir flashed back to what he originally had thought was his only possible environment: a bleak, gray landscape that was sparse of food and full of struggle. He now knew to look beyond his surroundings to all things that were possible. He briefly imagined what future adventures lay ahead, but remained in awe of the adventure he had just experienced. He had learned to guide his elephant. They had made progress, and the world had changed before their very eyes.

Here before Adir was a sight that left him breathless— and it appeared in a way he had never imagined. In his dreams, he envisioned arriving at the Oasis on a bright, sunny day. He fantasized about all the wildlife teeming with energy around the Oasis pond. Yet in this quiet night, his dream came true like a gentle breeze delivering a distant notion. Adir was amazed at how dreams do come true, but rarely in the way they are envisioned.

From Adir's perch on Elgo's head, he could see the many slumbering creatures of the Oasis. He saw zebras and giraffes asleep amidst the trees, and birds nesting upon elephants that looked remarkably like Elgo.

"Look, Elgo," he whispered, "your family . . ."

Deep in his bones, Adir knew it would be only a matter of time before he found his fellow ants. When he did, he would be the best ant he could possibly be. He would be a leader worth following, and he would teach them all he had learned on this amazing journey. He would teach them leadership for the self.

The ant and the elephant, both of whom had struggled for so long, took a deep breath in synchronicity. Then the ant said to his dear elephant friend, "The Oasis . . . We made it . . . Elgo, we're home!" *

• • •

---

* The End.

Afterword

Have you ever wondered why your best efforts can bring results that you had no conscious intention of producing? Do you ever marvel at the self-destructive patterns of other people and wonder, why? This dilemma frustrates most men and women and has been an obsession for practically my entire life. I have stayed in jobs I did not like. I have ended up in relationships that were horrible for my self-esteem. I have said yes to activities that immediately set me up to dread the event. I have intended to make more money, but remained broke. I have intended to create a better lot in life, but remained frustrated.

All this changed on November 12, 1992. Dr. Lee Pulos gave a speech in the areas of psychology and personal growth. At one point in the speech, he related a statistic based on fascinating scientific research: At birth, humans have approximately 120 billion glial cells, active neurons in the brain. Over time, through a natural process called pruning, unused neurons become dormant. As adults, we each end up with about ten billion active neurons available for conscious and subconscious brain activity.

Dr. Pulos revealed that in one second of time, the conscious mind uses about two thousand neurons. In that same second, the subconscious mind uses four billion neurons. This bears repeating: in *one second*, the subconscious mind uses four billion neurons. This means that every second, there are two thousand neurons making conscious decisions and *four billion* neurons making subconscious decisions. Now, ask yourself: "Who's in control?" Is it your conscious mind or your subconscious mind? Is it the ant or the elephant making decisions?

111

From 1988 to 1992, I used mental training techniques to reach the Olympic Winter Games and participate in the speed skiing competition. In November 1992, Dr. Lee Pulos revealed the answer that explained the enormous potential that exists in our subconscious minds. Drawing on my experience training for the Olympics, and prompted further by the important points emphasized by Dr. Pulos, I embarked on a path to define and maximize human potential.

This journey has expanded into the corporate arena. With my business consulting firm, Be Invinceable Group, I have made it a focus to align peak performers with specific corporate objectives. We uncover ways for business people to ignite their vision and execute strategies to eclipse their competition. It has become clear that to do all this, we need a book about peak performance and alignment. How can leaders, managers and employees reach their true potential? *The Ant and the Elephant* is the result of this quest.

This book's intention is to make a difference in your life and in the business of life. It is a small book, easy and quick to read for a purpose. In our world of uncertainty, combined with a seemingly increased time crunch, we are more often in reaction mode and less often in strategy mode. Although *The Ant and the Elephant* is designed to be an entertaining allegory, it contains powerful strategic tools that you can use to create peak performance, both personally and professionally.

Conventional wisdom says we control our own destinies. Yet, this wisdom stops at appreciating that the mind is more than just a conscious tool. Anything below consciousness is relegated to the realm of the mysterious. Practical approaches are somewhat rare. In this story, Adir the ant is a metaphor for your conscious mind. The elephant represents the subconscious. Until the ant can learn to lead and guide his subconscious, he will not be able to attain his goal.

I have yet to meet a person who does not admit to having at least a little disconnection between "his ant and his elephant." Since this book is in your hands, it is clear that you are also dedicated to finding new solutions to age-old problems and challenges. You see, this book was written just for you, the people you work with and the folks you care about most in life. *The Ant and the Elephant* is designed to help leaders understand themselves and the challenges they face. It is a book that will literally change the outcomes that organizations have, just by reading and applying the simple strategies herein. *The Ant and the Elephant* is designed to align your ant and your elephant.

You and I are more than our respective "ants" can conceive. Just like the four billion neurons in your subconscious mind that you might scarcely be aware of, you are sitting on an elephant of potential. Harness this potential with each employee at your company, and you will have the collective power of a herd of elephants driving toward a common goal.

Each of us is a leader with the responsibility to understand and internalize this common goal—our collective "oasis," if you will. The power within, aligned with the power of the many is equivalent to a tiny ant guiding a mighty elephant. Our oasis of satisfaction and fulfillment is our reward.

The **power within**, aligned with the **power of the many**, is **equivalent** to a **tiny ant** guiding a **mighty elephant**.

Use this book as your guide. Use it to help guide others. Remember these five Cs to build peak performance and sustain team alignment toward the goal:

1 | Clarify your vision.

Make fear your friend, not your master. You don't know what you don't know. Open your mind to discover possibilities that may not be obvious at the time. Zero in on a goal that has a depth of meaning. The journey has to be worth taking.

ACTION: Find the *elephant buzz*. Find the emotion that ignites the vision. Inspire your team through emotion. Never underestimate the power of emotion.

2 | Commit to cultivating positive dominant thoughts.

Shift beliefs, attitudes and truths so they are in alignment with your vision. Envision having the goal, rather than merely wanting the goal.

ACTION: Stay the course. Change is gradual. Remember the *Drops in the Bucket* to avoid frustration. Learn to delay gratification.

3 | Consistently focus on performance.

Experience the goal as though it were happening right now. Show your gratitude consistently.

ACTION: Use gold dot reminders. Gold dots are triggers for goals that have emotions tied to them. The personal gold dot must align with the gold dot of the team.

4 | Strengthen confidence.

Frustration will lead to negative thoughts. Negative thoughts fuel more negativity. This negativity can be a pattern that destroys confidence. No two thoughts can occupy the mind at the same time. Replace negativity with positive, confident thoughts.

ACTION: Institute pattern busters. Once you recognize yourself or your team playing out the pattern of negativity, interrupt the pattern by saying, "Thank you, but that is not part of my vision. My vision is . . ." Experience the vision in detail.

5 | Control the response to any situation.

Unforeseen circumstances will arise. Expect the unexpected. Anticipate your response to challenges as well as your team's.

ACTION: Use flash cards. Design flash cards that detail stressful scenarios. Mentally experience handling these stressful situations with ease.

115

Do this, and Adir, Elgo and I will see you at the Oasis!
Vince Poscente

Credits

Writing a fictional tale with substantive non-fiction content is one of the hardest things I have ever done. As men never experience giving birth, it seems that a two-year gestation period for a book is as close as I'll come to having a baby. And not surprisingly, I have many "midwives" to thank.

To the "Virtual R & D Team," thank you for all your input during the creation of this book. About sixty of you gave feedback on the first draft of the book. Some of you gave a simple thumbs up, and others spent hours providing me with specific ideas on how to improve the book in general. For particularly notable input and suggestions, I owe a special thank you to Yossi Ghinsberg, Jamie Clarke, Amanda Gore, Steve Cox, Steve Straus, Cary Mullen, Christa Haberstock and Steven Poscente. Additional heartfelt gratitude goes to Gail Melvin, Patrick Walsh, Marjorie Snaith, Rand Stagen, Julie Grau, Dale Irvin, Shep Hyken, Cindy Rodella, Barb Bilyeu, Linda Swindling, Paul Frazer, Carol Apelt and Val Majeau. Another thank you to my good friend Dale Leicht—you're a wonderful sounding board.

Thank you to Janice Phelps and Susan Hayes for your initial editing suggestions. To David Cottrell at CornerStone Leadership Institute, thank you for always being ready with a supportive word and a guiding, helping hand.

From Greenleaf Book Group, thank you to Nicole Hirsh. You're an editing angel. Only a talented editor could do what you did. The book has been through a number of iterations. Nicole, thank you for helping to polish it so it gleamed. Also, a special thank you goes to Meg La Borde. Your literary talents and instinct for the book world made finalizing this book fun!

Thank you to all the Greenleaf people who had a hand in the final edits, layout and design: Francine Smith for your innovative layout and Mark Dame of Dame Creative, for your talents on the cover. Thank you to Clint Greenleaf for your support. I'll never forget your first comments, "This is gold, baby . . . *Gold!*"

Thanks also to my staff at Be Invinceable Group, led by Brian Kennedy and Linda Perez, who made sure I had the space needed to complete this work. Your dedication, commitment and professionalism inspire me. Our consulting team would not be as successful without you. To everyone at Complete Marketing Incorporated, thank you very much for your expertise in the speaker management world. Karen Harris, Mylnda Skopyk, Mary Ross and Kristina Mullen, you make my job a delight.

A blanket thank you goes to all the clients I have had the privilege to work with over the last ten years. I have either spoken to or consulted with more than 750 corporations or associations, and to spend time with more than 600,000 people around the global community is an honor.

Finally, and most importantly, I would like to thank my family: my wife, Michelle, and children, Max, Alexia and Isabella. You find yourselves sharing me with eighty clients each year. Between writing, speaking and business consulting, our time is precious, and I deeply appreciate your unconditional love.

the ant and the

ELEPHANT

Workshop-in-a-Box

by Vince Poscente

Olympian and Peak Performance Strategist

Transform Individual Performance

Take Your Entire Team Through the *Ant and the Elephant* Experience

Now you can bring the powerful learning experience found in the best-selling business book, *The Ant and the Elephant* to your entire team or organization. The Workshop-in-a-Box contains everything you need to deliver a fun, impactful training module at your company. Complete with an instructional Facilitator Guide, five Participant Guides, PowerPoint presentation, hardcover book, Keynote DVD, Gold Dot Starter Kit, and a special bonus mouse pad, the Application Kit will equip you with the necessary knowledge base and tools to lead an intact team or workgroup to an understanding of the power of self-leadership to transform personal and workplace performance.

Workshop-in-a-Box $495.95
Additional Participant Guides (5 pack) $45.00

To Order: 800-791-2078 or go to **www.antandelephant.com**

The Workshop-in-a-Box is a complete program with all the tools you need to lead a high-impact training workshop.

Facilitator Guide
60 pages
Includes facilitator checklist, notes, exercises, and a complete script.

Workshop-in-a-Box includes
- Compete Facilitator Guide
- AE PowerPoint (CD)
- AE Participant Guides (5)
- AE Hardcover Book
- AE Mouse Pad
- Vince Poscente Keynote (DVD)
- Gold Dot Starter Kit

5 Participant Guides
Includes workshop agenda, individual exercises, and other resources. Additional guides can be purchased separately.

Complete PowerPoint presentation
Includes 72 full-color slides synchronized with facilitator and participant guides.

Vince Poscente DVD
The recommended starting point for the *Ant and the Elephant* workshop.

The Ant and the Elephant hardcover book
Quantity discounts available. Ideal for pre- or post-event reading.

Gold Dot Starter Kit
A powerful tool to help clarify your vision and guide your desired results.

Special Bonus
The Ant and the Elephant Mouse Pad
Each kit includes a special mouse pad that's a great reminder of timeless truths.